BACKCOUNTRY FOODIE

ULTRALIGHT RECIPES FOR OUTDOOR EXPLORERS

AARON OWENS MAYHEW, MS, RDN, CD

Cover photograph by Chris Mayhew

Book cover and interior design by Natalie Broussard - www.nataliethedesigner.com

Copy editing by Kelsie Hunter, RD, CD and Michaela Rush, MS, RD, CD

Wedding photo by Jamie VanBuhler of Visual Life Photography – www.jvanbuhler.com

If you have any questions or comments regarding this book, please email us at aaron@backcountryfoodie.com.

To my Christopher,

It is because of you that this book exists. You have supported my over-the-top dreams and aspirations and cheered for me throughout the entire journey. It's not every day that a girl meets a guy that is supportive of her quitting her job and going for a long walk to figure out what will come next in her life. Because of that long walk, and you, I not only found a new passion for food and nutrition but have been able to share my love for it with other people through this book. I am grateful that you will forever be a part of my adventures to come.

This book is dedicated to you.

CONTENTS

How to Use This Book

You will find the following graphics listed in the sidebar of each recipe allowing you to quickly scan the cookbook for recipes meeting your personal dietary needs and meal prep style.

 Cook
Meals that require the use of a stove to heat water.

 Vegetarian
Meals that are free of meat, but potentially contain dairy and/or eggs.

 No-Cook
Ready-to-eat meals or meals that require only cold water.

 Vegan
Meals that are plant-based and free of meat, dairy and/or eggs.

 Cold Soak
Meals that require the addition of water and are then allowed to rehydrate over several hours.

**Times provided for cold soak meals are estimates. It is recommended that you test these recipes prior to use in the backcountry to determine exact times according to your preferences.

 Vegan Option
The primary recipe listed may be vegetarian but substitutions listed within the recipe allow for a vegan alternative.

 Nut-free
Meals that are free of peanuts and tree nuts.

**Trace amounts of peanuts and tree nuts and/or contamination with peanuts and tree nuts cannot be guaranteed.

 Gluten-free
Meals that are free of gluten.

 Gluten-free Option
The primary recipe listed may include gluten but suggested substitutions allow for a gluten-free alternative.

**Trace amount of gluten and/or contamination with gluten cannot be guaranteed.

Nutrition Information and Substitutions

Nutrition information provided is representative of the recipes outlined. Within each section of the cookbook, the recipes are organized from highest to lowest calories per ounce (kcal/oz). Substitution suggestions are provided for recipes where feature ingredients may not be suitable for all diets. Nutrition information is not currently available for substitutions.

Common Conversions

15 mL	1/2 oz
3 tsp	1 Tbsp
2 Tbsp	1/8 cup
8 Tbsp	1/2 cup
16 Tbsp	1 cup
28 grams	1 oz dry weight

Shelf Life

Shelf life of recipes included in this cookbook can vary greatly, as there are many individual factors that can impact shelf life. Shelf life is affected by sunlight, moisture, exposure to oxygen, storage temperature, and fat content of the food.

It is recommended that you prepare test versions of the recipes and store them for various time periods to determine shelf life where you live to account for variations in climate. Keeping a simple log book of inventory is an easy way to track this. This would be a good practice for all recipes in this book.

To maximize shelf life, consider the following recommendations:

- Reduce exposure to light by storing recipes in a dark location such as a pantry, closet, or dark colored plastic tote.

- Reduce oxygen exposure by vacuum sealing recipes. Zip-top bags are not air tight. Adding an oxygen absorber to vacuum sealed or zip-top bags is not necessary when vacuum sealing meals.

- Prevent mold by ensuring all ingredients and packing supplies are completely dry when preparing and storing recipes. Moisture absorbers are not necessary when vacuum sealing meals.

- Prevent bacterial growth by thoroughly washing your hands and cooking surfaces before and during the preparation of food for long-term storage. Wearing gloves will further reduce risk of bacterial growth. Wearing a hair net is also advised, especially if you will be sharing your meals with friends in the backcountry!

- Store meals in a cool place to extend shelf life, ideally below room temperature (70 ° F or 21 ° C). If space allows, storing meals in the freezer is ideal.

- Reduce risk for spoilage by using the freshest ingredients (ie. a freshly opened container of nuts instead of nuts purchased from bulk bins). Since Backcountry Foodie meals are generally higher in fat, and higher fat content can lead to food spoilage, these recipes are meant to be eaten, not stored long-term. If properly prepared with food safety precautions in mind, the majority of the recipes should remain shelf stable for up to six months.

Ingredients

All nutrition calculations assume the use of the products specified. Brand and product substitutions may be used at your own discretion with slight variations to the finished product as well as nutrition content.

You will find the URL for a listing of products used in this book on the following page of each recipe. There you will find links to various product pages. Disclosure: Some of the links may be associated with affiliate programs with Backcountry Foodie LLC earning a small commission if you choose to purchase the product. This will occur at no cost to you.

Backcountry Foodie cannot guarantee the accuracy of the nutrition information listed as manufacturer ingredient lists may change or be incomplete without our knowledge.

Dehydrated vs. Freeze-dried Ingredients

Dehydrated ingredients may be used in place of freeze-dried ingredients, however, please note that some dehydrated ingredients may not fully rehydrate and will remain crunchy. If using dehydrated ingredients, expect the rehydration process to take longer than would be required if using freeze-dried ingredients.

Be aware that dehydrated ingredients do weigh more than their freeze-dried counterparts which increases the total weight of the meal and reduces caloric density. Freeze-dried ingredients are used in this book as the focus is to prepare recipes that weigh the least amount possible while providing maximum nutrition.

Safe Dehydration of Foods

There are a variety of resources and forums online providing guidelines and tips for safely dehydrating food at home. It is important to use a dehydrator with a temperature gauge and to verify that the temperature is accurate when drying food. Increasing the temperature above what is recommended can potentially result in case hardening. This occurs when the outside of the food dries before the inside. Drying times vary based on thickness of the food, humidity, water content of the food and wattage of the dehydrator. The United States Department of Agriculture (USDA) web page and local Department of Agriculture offices are great resources when learning how to safely dehydrate food.

Recommendations:

Food Type	Temperature
Jerky	130-140 degrees, after being heated to 160-165 degrees prior to dehydration
Fruit and Vegetables	125 degrees
Nuts	125 degrees
Beans	115 degrees
Fresh Herbs	90-110 degrees

Recipe Weight

The written and actual weight of recipes may vary slightly due to differences between household measures and measurements determined by commercial recipe software used to write this cookbook.

Please report any noticeable discrepancies to aaron@backcountryfoodie.com.

Field Prep Time

The field prep times provided for recipes in this book are based on cooking time at sea level. Altitude will most notably affect the recipes which require cooking, as altitude affects the boiling point of water. The higher the altitude, the lower the boiling point of water. When water boils at lower temperatures, it takes longer for foods to cook.

For recipes that require less than 20 minutes of cook time at sea level, add 1 minute of cooking time for every 1000 feet above sea level.

For recipes that require more than 20 minutes of cook time at sea level, add 2 minutes of cooking time for each 1000 feet above sea level.

High altitude areas (>2500 ft) are prone to low humidity, which can cause the moisture in foods to evaporate more quickly during cooking. Covering foods during cooking will help retain moisture.

When adding additional cook time to account for altitude be sure to plan for extra fuel.

Elevation	Cooking Time
Sea Level (0 feet)	10 minutes
2,000 feet	12 minutes
5,000 feet	15 minutes
7,500 feet	18 minutes
10,000 feet	20 minutes
20,000 feet	30 minutes

Adding Oil to Meals

Unless you're following a ketogenic or low carb/high fat diet, the recipes included in this cookbook are likely to be higher in fat than those typically consumed at home or during previous backcountry trips. When transitioning to an ultralight diet in the backcountry, consider transitioning slowly due to potential changes in stool patterns as a result of high fat intake.

For those that are long-distance hikers, consider leaving out the additional oil for the first 1-2 weeks and increase the oil content as tolerated to meet the final calorie goal as the trip progresses.

Those that are only spending a few days in the backcountry may be less likely to notice changes in stool patterns. The additional oil may not be necessary due to the lower calorie needs over the course of shorter trips.

Portion Sizes

Many of the portion sizes in this cookbook are intended to satisfy the appetite of those spending time in the backcountry for extended periods such as thru hikes and/or expeditions.

For shorter trips, consider cutting the recipes in half as the portion sizes may be excessive if combined with snacks over the course of the day.

For thru hiking or outdoor adventures resulting in high energy expenditure, recipes may need to be doubled to account for increased caloric needs.

What To Expect When Reading This Cookbook

- Recipes that are included in Backcountry Foodie's own personal meal plans and those created for her clients.

- Recipes that provide enough protein for an endurance athlete (1.5-1.8 g/kg). This protein content will potentially improve performance by encouraging muscle recovery.

- Recipes that are designed to be prepared within minutes at home allowing you to spend more time outdoors.

- Recipes that cook quickly in the backcountry allowing you to spend less time in camp in the morning, continue moving mid-day, and eat quickly at the end of the day to maximize time available for sleep and muscle recovery.

- Recipes that require minimal amounts of water. This helps reduce the water weight carried in your pack, the need to camp near a water source, and fuel required to heat the water.

- Recipes with high fiber content that aid in slowed digestion, allowing you to feel satiated for an extended period of time. High fiber content of meals can also help address potential concern for constipation if meals are consumed for an extended period of time such as a thru hike. Many convenience foods oftentimes consumed by thru hikers do not serve as an adequate source of fiber.

- Recipes that are high in fat to serve as a slow burning fuel that will help sustain your energy level over the course of the day.

- Recipes that are low in weight and volume reducing your total pack weight and space needed to store the food in your pack, kayak, saddle bags, etc.

- Recipes that work well when using bear canisters as they mold to the sides of the can and fill in the empty spaces.

How To Use The Label Templates

On the back of each recipe you will find the link to access the downloadable label file for that recipe. You can type the url manually, or use a barcode scanner app on your mobile device to scan the included QR code to be taken directly to the download page.

You can use these label files to print labels for the recipe. These templates will save you time by eliminating the need to hand-write what is included and/or the preparation instructions on the bags or containers containing the meals prepared.

Garlic Parmesan Ramen

Directions: Add 8 oz hot/cold water to cover noodles. Let stand to rehydrate. Consume or properly discard broth. Add dry ingredients packet and 4 Tbsp olive oil. Stir and enjoy!

Ingredients: ramen noodles, parmesan cheese, parsley, garlic powder, black pepper, salt

Nutrition: 982 kcal (158 kcal/oz), 21 g protein, 53 g carbohydrate, 3 g fiber, 2 g total sugars, 78 g fat

Net wt: 6.2 oz (including oil)   **Exp. Date:** _____

www.backcountryfoodie.com

Example label

The templates are designed to be used with Avery 2" x 4" shipping address labels 8163 (inkjet) or Avery 2" x 4" shipping address labels 5263 (laser).

A blank space is also included on the labels to write in the expiration date of the meal based on the recipe used. We recommend doing this so that you can consume the oldest recipes first to avoid food waste and/or opening a meal in the backcountry that has expired. We're sure you will agree that there's nothing worse than opening a meal that's not edible at the end of a long day in the backcountry.

When printing the labels, be sure to choose "Print Actual Size" as the labels will not print correctly if this option is not chosen.

Terms of Use

The recipes in this book are provided for informational purposes only, and are not intended to constitute nutrition advice. Backcountry Foodie LLC cannot guarantee that the recipes will be nutritionally complete, appropriate, or safe for any pre-existing medical conditions. Backcountry Foodie recommends that the reader consult with its personal healthcare provider for advice regarding whether the nutrition content of the recipes is appropriate.

BREAKFAST

Citrus Pecan Cream Cheese

INGREDIENTS

2/3 cup cream cheese powder

4 tsp honey crystals

1/4 cup pecans, chopped

1 tsp dried orange peel

AT HOME DIRECTIONS

1. Put all ingredients in a bag or container to be used in the backcountry.

2. Pair with bagel chips or crackers of choice.

FIELD DIRECTIONS

1. Add 1 oz cold water and stir well.

2. Cream cheese will thicken and orange flavor will intensity

   if allowed to stand before consuming.

3. Stir, spread on bagel chips or crackers and enjoy!

HOME PREP
Mix Dry Ingred.

HOME PREP TIME
4 Min

FIELD PREP
No Cook

FIELD PREP TIME
2 Min

TOTAL SERVINGS
1

WEIGHT/ SERVING
3.7 oz

	KCAL/OZ	CALORIES	PROTEIN	CARBS	FIBER	SUGAR	FAT
Nutrition Info PER SERVING	182	675	3g	26g	3g	24g	62g

Download the Label File for

Citrus Pecan Cream Cheese

Directions: Add 1 oz cold water or to desired consistency. Stir and let stand. Cream cheese will thicken with time. Stir and enjoy!

Ingredients: cream cheese powder, honey crystals, pecans, dehydrated orange peel

Nutrition: 675 kcal (182 kcal/oz), 3 g protein, 26 g carbohydrate, 3 g fiber, 24 g total sugars, 62 g fat

Net wt: 3.7 oz   Exp. Date: _____

www.backcountryfoodie.com

To download this label template, visit

https://www.backcountryfoodie.com/labels/citrus-pecan-cream-cheese.pdf

or scan this barcode:

To find URL links for ingredients used, visit

https://backcountryfoodie.com/ingredients/

Granola with Yogurt & Berries

INGREDIENTS

1 cup granola

1 cup freeze dried yogurt drops

2 Tbsp freeze dried blueberries

2 Tbsp freeze dried strawberries

Substitutions:

Various granola brands maybe used but be aware that granola comes in varying fat content. Choose the highest calorie option when preparing this ultralight recipe.

AT HOME DIRECTIONS

1. Put yogurt in food processor and grind into powder.
2. Put yogurt and berries into bag or storage container to be used in the backcountry.
3. Put granola in second bag to be stored inside the primary container to prevent clumping with yogurt.

FIELD DIRECTIONS

1. Remove granola bag.
2. Add 8 oz cold water to yogurt and berries bag or to desired consistency.
3. Stir and let stand until rehydrated.
4. Add granola to yogurt and berry mix and enjoy!

VEGETARIAN

NUT-FREE

NO-COOK

HOME PREP

Mix Dry Ingred.

HOME PREP TIME

5 Min

FIELD PREP

No Cook

FIELD PREP TIME

2 Min

TOTAL SERVINGS

1

WEIGHT/ SERVING

5.7 oz

Nutrition Info PER SERVING	KCAL/OZ	CALORIES	PROTEIN	CARBS	FIBER	SUGAR	FAT
	143	817	36g	106g	9g	64g	31g

Download the Label File for

Granola with Yogurt and Berries

Directions: Add 8 oz cold cold water to yogurt and berries mix. Let stand. Add granola once rehydrated. Stir and enjoy!

Ingredients: granola, freeze dried yogurt, freeze dried blueberries, freeze dried strawberries

Nutrition: 817 kcal (143 kcal/oz), 36 g protein, 106 g carbohydrate, 9 g fiber, 64 Total Sugars, 31 g fat

Net wt: 3.8 oz   Exp. Date: _____

www.backcountryfoodie.com

To download this label template, visit

https://www.backcountryfoodie.com/labels/granola-and-yogurt-with-berries.pdf

or scan this barcode:

To find URL links for ingredients used, visit

https://backcountryfoodie.com/ingredients/

Raisin Pecan Ramen

INGREDIENTS

1 package ramen noodles

1/8 cup raisins

1/4 cup pecans, chopped

1 Tbsp brown sugar

1/4 tsp cinnamon

1 Tbsp coconut oil

Substitutions

Rice ramen noodles may be used as gluten-free alternative.

AT HOME DIRECTIONS

1. Discard ramen noodle spice packet.

2. Put noodles in a bag or container to be used in the backcountry.

3. Put remaining dry ingredients in second bag to be stored with the noodles

4. Pack 1 Tbsp (1 – 0.5 oz packet) coconut oil, per serving, in a leakproof container to be added to the meal when consumed. Recommend double bagging the oil in the event there is a leak.

FIELD DIRECTIONS

1. Remove raisin mix packet.

2. Add 8 oz hot/cold water or enough water to cover the noodles.

3. Let stand until rehydrated.

4. Consume or properly discard the noodle broth to practice the Leave No Trace principle.

5. Add raisin mix packet and 1 Tbsp (1 – 0.5 oz packet) coconut oil to noodles.

6. Stir well and enjoy!

GLUTEN-FREE OPTION

COOK

COLD SOAK

HOME PREP

Mix Dry Ingred.

HOME PREP TIME

3 Min

FIELD PREP

Cook, Cold Soak

FIELD PREP TIME

6-30 Min

TOTAL SERVINGS

1

WEIGHT/ SERVING

5.7 oz

	KCAL/OZ	CALORIES	PROTEIN	CARBS	FIBER	SUGAR	FAT
Nutrition Info PER SERVING	140	798	12g	85g	6g	28g	48g

Download the Label File for

Raisin Pecan Ramen

Directions: Remove raisin mix packet. Add 8 oz hot/cold water to noodles. Let stand to rehydrate. Add raisin mix packet and 1 Tbsp coconut oil. Stir and enjoy!

Ingredients: ramen noodles, raisins, pecans, brown sugar, cinnamon

Nutrition: 798 kcal (140 kcal/oz), 12 g protein, 85 g carbohydrate, 6 g fiber, 28 g total sugars, 48 g fat

Net wt: 5.7 oz (including oil)   **Exp. Date:** _____

www.backcountryfoodie.com

To download this label template, visit

https://www.backcountryfoodie.com/labels/raisin-pecan-ramen.pdf

or scan this barcode:

To find URL links for ingredients used, visit

https://backcountryfoodie.com/ingredients/

Fruity Breakfast Grits

INGREDIENTS

2 packets of instant grits

1/8 cup freeze dried strawberries

1/8 cup freeze dried pineapple

2 Tbsp coconut milk powder

1 Tbsp coconut oil

AT HOME DIRECTIONS

1. Put all dry ingredients in a bag or container to be used in the backcountry.

2. Pack 1 Tbsp (1 – 0.5 oz packet) coconut oil, per serving, in a leakproof container to be added to the meal when consumed. Recommend double bagging the oil in the event there is a leak.

FIELD DIRECTIONS

1. Add 6 oz hot water to bag.

2. Stir and let stand until rehydrated.

3. Add 1 tbsp (1 – 0.5 oz packet) coconut oil to the bag.

4. Stir and enjoy.

GLUTEN-FREE

NUT-FREE

COOK

HOME PREP

Mix Dry Ingred.

HOME PREP TIME

5 Min

FIELD PREP

Cook

FIELD PREP TIME

3 Min

TOTAL SERVINGS

1

WEIGHT/ SERVING

3.1 oz

Nutrition Info PER SERVING	KCAL/OZ	CALORIES	PROTEIN	CARBS	FIBER	SUGAR	FAT
	138	428	6g	52g	3g	4g	21g

Download the Label File for

Fruity Breakfast Grits

Directions: Add 4 oz hot water to bag. Stir and let stand. Add 1 Tbsp coconut oil. Stir and enjoy!

Ingredients: instant grits, strawberries, pineapple, coconut milk powder

Nutrition: 428 kcal (138 kcal/oz), 6 g protein, 52 g carbohydrate, 3 g fiber, 4 g total sugars, 21 g fat

Net wt: 3.1 oz (including oil)   **Exp. Date:** _____

www.backcountryfoodie.com

To download this label template, visit

https://www.backcountryfoodie.com/labels/fruity-breakfast-grits.pdf

or scan this barcode:

To find URL links for ingredients used, visit

https://backcountryfoodie.com/ingredients/

Cherry Almond Milk Oatmeal

INGREDIENTS

1/2 cup instant rolled oats

2 Tbsp freeze dried sweet cherries

2 Tbsp almonds, sliced

3 Tbsp almond milk powder

1/2 tsp cinnamon

1 tsp brown sugar

1 Tbsp coconut oil

Note:

Asian markets typically sell a variety of nut powders if unable to find almond milk powder online.

AT HOME DIRECTIONS

1. Put all ingredients in a bag or container to be used in the backcountry.

2. Pack 1 Tbsp (1 – 0.5 oz packet) coconut oil, per serving, in a leakproof container to be added to the meal when consumed. Recommend double bagging the oil in the event there is a leak.

FIELD DIRECTIONS

1. Add 4 oz hot water or to desired consistency.

2. Stir well and let stand allowing the cherries to rehydrate.

3. Add 1 Tbsp (1 – 0.5 oz packet) coconut oil.

4. Stir and enjoy!

HOME PREP

Mix Dry Ingred.

HOME PREP TIME

3 Min

FIELD PREP

Cook

FIELD PREP TIME

3 Min

TOTAL SERVINGS

1

WEIGHT/ SERVING

4.0 oz

Nutrition **Info** PER SERVING	KCAL/OZ	CALORIES	PROTEIN	CARBS	FIBER	SUGAR	FAT
	136	543	13g	59g	7g	12g	30g

Download the Label File for

Cherry Almond Milk Oatmeal

Directions: Add 4 oz hot water, stir and let stand. Add 1 Tbsp coconut oil after rehydrated. Stir and enjoy!

Ingredients: instant rolled oats, freeze dried sweet cherries, shredded unsweetened coconut, almonds, almond milk powder, cinnamon, brown sugar

Nutrition: 543 kcal (136 kcal/oz), 13 g protein, 59 g carbohydrate, 7 g fiber, 12 g total sugars, 30 g fat

Net wt: 4 oz (including oil)   Exp. Date: _____

www.backcountryfoodie.com

To download this label template, visit

https://www.backcountryfoodie.com/labels/cherry-almond-milk-oatmeal.pdf

or scan this barcode:

To find URL links for ingredients used, visit

https://backcountryfoodie.com/ingredients/

Backcountry Cheese Grits

INGREDIENTS

2 packets instant grits

1/2 cup whole milk powder

1 Tbsp egg white powder

2 Tbsp freeze dried parmesan cheese

1/4 tsp black pepper

1 Tbsp olive oil

AT HOME DIRECTIONS

1. Put all dry ingredients in a bag or container to be used in the backcountry.

2. Pack 1 Tbsp olive oil, per serving, in a leakproof container to be added to the meal when consumed. Recommend double bagging the oil in the event there is a leak.

FIELD DIRECTIONS

1. Add 8 oz hot water or to desired consistency.

2. Stir well allowing cheese to melt.

3. Add 1 Tbsp olive oil.

4. Stir and enjoy!

HOME PREP

Mix Dry Ingred.

HOME PREP TIME

5 Min

FIELD PREP

Cook

FIELD PREP TIME

3 Min

TOTAL SERVINGS

1

WEIGHT/ SERVING

6.1 oz

Nutrition Info PER SERVING

KCAL/OZ	CALORIES	PROTEIN	CARBS	FIBER	SUGAR	FAT
136	827	47g	67g	2g	23g	37g

Download the Label File for

Backcountry Cheese Grits

Directions: Add 8 oz hot water and mix well allowing the cheese to melt. Add 1 Tbsp olive oil. Stir and enjoy!

Ingredients: instant grits, whole milk powder, egg white powder, freeze dried parmesan cheese, black pepper

Nutrition: 827 kcal (136 kcal/oz), 47 g protein, 67 g carbohydrate, 2 g fiber, 23 total sugars, 37 g fat

Net wt: 6.1 oz (including oil)   **Exp. Date:** _____

www.backcountryfoodie.com

To download this label template, visit

https://www.backcountryfoodie.com/labels/backcountry-cheese-grits.pdf

or scan this barcode:

To find URL links for ingredients used, visit

https://backcountryfoodie.com/ingredients/

Lemon Blueberry Oatmeal

INGREDIENTS

1 cup instant oatmeal

1/3 cup whole milk powder

1/2 cup freeze dried blueberries

1/4 cup almonds, sliced

1 Tbsp brown sugar

2 tsp honey crystals

1 packet True Lemon® powder

1 Tbsp coconut oil

AT HOME DIRECTIONS

1. Put all dry ingredients in bag or container to be used in the backcountry.

2. Pack 1 Tbsp (1 – 0.5 oz packet) coconut oil, per serving, in a leakproof container to be added to the meal when consumed. Recommend double bagging the oil in the event there is a leak.

FIELD DIRECTIONS

1. Add 8 oz hot water or to desired consistency.

2. Stir and let stand allowing blueberries to rehydrate.

3. Add 1 Tbsp (1 – 0.5 oz packet) coconut oil.

4. Stir and enjoy!

HOME PREP

Mix Dry Ingred.

HOME PREP TIME

3 Min

FIELD PREP

Cook

FIELD PREP TIME

2 Min

TOTAL SERVINGS

1

WEIGHT/ SERVING

6.8 oz

	KCAL/OZ	CALORIES	PROTEIN	CARBS	FIBER	SUGAR	FAT
Nutrition Info PER SERVING	132	897	26g	105g	12g	45g	42g

Download the Label File for

Lemon Blueberry Oatmeal

Directions: Add 8 oz hot water, stir and let stand. Add 1 Tbsp coconut oil after rehydrated and mix well.

Ingredients: instant oatmeal, whole mlk powder, freeze-dried blueberries, almonds, brown sugar, honey crystals, lemon powder

Nutrition: 897 kcal (132 kcal/oz), 26 g protein, 105 g carbohydrate, 12 g fiber, 45 g total sugars, 42 g fat

Net wt: 6.8 oz (including oil)   Exp. Date: _____

www.backcountryfoodie.com

To download this label template, visit

https://www.backcountryfoodie.com/labels/lemon-blueberry-oatmeal.pdf

or scan this barcode:

To find URL links for ingredients used, visit

https://backcountryfoodie.com/ingredients/

Strawberry Coconut Almond Oatmeal

INGREDIENTS

1/2 cup instant oatmeal

1/8 cup whole milk powder

1/4 cup freeze dried strawberries

1 Tbsp honey powder

1 Tbsp shredded unsweetened coconut

2 Tbsp almonds, sliced

1 Tbsp coconut oil

AT HOME DIRECTIONS

1. Put all ingredients in a bag or container used in the backcountry.

2. Pack 1 Tbsp (1 – 0.5 oz packet) coconut oil, per serving, in a leakproof container to be added to the meal when consumed. Recommend double bagging the oil in the event there is a leak.

FIELD DIRECTIONS

1. Add 4 oz hot water or to desired consistency.

2. Stir and let stand allowing strawberries to rehydrate.

3. Add 1 Tbsp (1 – 0.5 oz packet) coconut oil.

4. Stir and enjoy!

VEGETARIAN

GLUTEN-FREE

COOK

HOME PREP

Mix Dry Ingred.

HOME PREP TIME

3 Min

FIELD PREP

Cook

FIELD PREP TIME

3 Min

TOTAL SERVINGS

1

WEIGHT/ SERVING

4.3 oz

Nutrition Info PER SERVING	KCAL/OZ	CALORIES	PROTEIN	CARBS	FIBER	SUGAR	FAT
	130	558	14g	62g	8g	26g	30g

Download the Label File for

Strawberry Coconut Almond Oatmeal

Directions: Add 4 oz hot water or to desired consistency. Add 1 Tbsp coconut oil. Stir and enjoy!

Ingredients: instant oatmeal, whole milk powder, freeze dried strawberries, honey powder, unsweetened shredded coconut, sliced almonds

Nutrition: 558 kcal (130 kcal/oz), 14 g protein, 62 g carbohydrate, 8 g fiber, 26 g total sugars, 30 g fat

Net wt: 4.3 oz (including oil)   Exp. Date: _____

www.backcountryfoodie.com

To download this label template, visit

https://www.backcountryfoodie.com/labels/strawberry-coconut-almond-oatmeal.pdf

or scan this barcode:

To find URL links for ingredients used, visit

https://backcountryfoodie.com/ingredients/

LUNCH & DINNER

Pine Nut Pesto Hummus

INGREDIENTS

1/2 cup dry hummus mix

1/8 cup pine nuts

1 tsp basil

1/8 cup parmesan cheese

1/4 tsp black pepper

3 Tbsp olive oil

Shelf life will be extended if single serving packets of parmesan cheese are added at time of consumption or the meal is frozen until consumed.

AT HOME DIRECTIONS

1. Put all ingredients in a bag or container to be used in the backcountry.
2. Pack 3 Tbsp olive oil, per serving, in a leakproof container to be added to the meal when consumed. Recommend double bagging the oil in the event there is a leak.

FIELD DIRECTIONS

1. Add 6 oz cold water or to desired consistency.
2. Stir and allow to rehydrate.
3. Add 3 Tbsp olive oil.
4. Stir and enjoy!

VEGETARIAN

GLUTEN-FREE

NO-COOK

HOME PREP
Mix Dry Ingred.

HOME PREP TIME
3 Min

FIELD PREP
No Cook

FIELD PREP TIME
2 Min

TOTAL SERVINGS
1

WEIGHT/ SERVING
4.8 oz

Nutrition Info PER SERVING

KCAL/OZ	CALORIES	PROTEIN	CARBS	FIBER	SUGAR	FAT
174	835	21g	39g	7g	.6g	69g

Download the Label File for

Pine Nut Pesto Hummus

Directions: Add 6 cold water or to desired consistency. Add 3 Tbsp olive oil. Stir and enjoy!

Ingredients: dry hummus mix, pine nuts, basil, parmesan cheese, black pepper

Nutrition: 835 kcal (174 kcal/oz), 21 g protein, 39 g carbohydrate, 7 g fiber, 0.6 g total sugars, 69 g fat

Net wt: 4.8 oz (including oil)   Exp. Date: _____

www.backcountryfoodie.com

To download this label template, visit

https://www.backcountryfoodie.com/labels/pine-nut-pesto-hummus.pdf

or scan this barcode:

To find URL links for ingredients used, visit

https://backcountryfoodie.com/ingredients/

Southwest Cheese Dip & Chips

INGREDIENTS

1/3 cup cream cheese powder

1/8 cup white cheddar cheese powder

1/4 tsp taco seasoning

1/2 tsp cumin, ground

2 oz bag Fritos® original corn chips

AT HOME DIRECTIONS

1. Put all dry ingredients directly into to the bag or container to be used in the backcountry.

2. Pair with 2 oz bag Fritos ® original corn chips.

FIELD DIRECTIONS

1. Add 1 oz cold water and stir well. Add less water if thicker spread preferred.

2. Dip chips and enjoy!

VEGETARIAN

GLUTEN-FREE

NUT-FREE

NO-COOK

HOME PREP

Mix Dry Ingred.

HOME PREP TIME

5 Min

FIELD PREP

No Cook

FIELD PREP TIME

5 Min

TOTAL SERVINGS

1

WEIGHT/ SERVING

3.8 oz

Nutrition Info PER SERVING	KCAL/OZ	CALORIES	PROTEIN	CARBS	FIBER	SUGAR	FAT
	163	618	8g	43g	2g	8g	45g

Download the Label File for

Southwest Cheese Dip with Chips

Directions: Add 1 oz cold water or to desired consistency. Stir and enjoy!

Ingredients: cream cheese powder, white cheddar cheese powder, taco seasoning, cumin, 2 oz bag Fritos® original corn chips

Nutrition: 618 kcal (163 kcal/oz), 8 g protein, 43 g carbohydrate, 2 g fiber, 8 g total sugars, 45 g fat

Net wt: 3.8 oz   **Exp. Date:** _____

www.backcountryfoodie.com

To download this label template, visit

https://www.backcountryfoodie.com/labels/southwest-cheese-dip-with-chips.pdf

or scan this barcode:

To find URL links for ingredients used, visit

https://backcountryfoodie.com/ingredients/

Parmesan Pesto Ramen

INGREDIENTS

1 package ramen noodles

1/8 cup parmesan cheese

1/8 cup pine nuts

1/8 tsp garlic powder

1 Tbsp dried basil

1/8 tsp salt

3 tbsp olive oil

Substitutions

Rice ramen noodles may be used as gluten-free alternative

Shelf life will be extended if single serving packets of parmesan cheese are added at time of consumption or the meal is frozen until consumed.

AT HOME DIRECTIONS

1. Discard ramen noodle spice packet.

2. Put noodles in a bag or container to be used in the backcountry.

3. Put remaining dry ingredients in a second bag to be stored inside the noodle bag.

4. Pack 3 Tbsp olive oil, per serving, in a leakproof container to be added to the meal when consumed. Recommend double bagging the oil in the event there is a leak.

FIELD DIRECTIONS

1. Remove the pesto packet.

2. Add 6 oz hot/cold water or enough to cover the noodles.

3. Let stand allowing noodles to rehydrate.

4. Consume or properly discard the noodle broth to practice the Leave No Trace principle.

5. Add pesto packet and 3 Tbsp olive oil to noodle bag.

6. Stir well and enjoy!

VEGETARIAN

GLUTEN-FREE OPTION

COOK

COLD SOAK

HOME PREP

Mix Dry Ingred.

HOME PREP TIME

3 Min

FIELD PREP

Cook, Cold Soak

FIELD PREP TIME

5-30 Min

TOTAL SERVINGS

1

WEIGHT/ SERVING

5.8 oz

Nutrition nfo PER SERVING	KCAL/OZ	CALORIES	PROTEIN	CARBS	FIBER	SUGAR	FAT
	163	946	18g	55g	5g	2g	74g

Download the Label File for

Parmesan Pesto Ramen

Directions: Remove pesto packet. Add 8 oz hot/cold water and let stand. Consume or properly discard broth. Add pesto packet and 4 Tbsp olive oil. Stir and enjoy!

Ingredients: ramen noodles, parmesan cheese, pine nuts, garlic powder, basil, salt

Nutrition: 946 kcal (163 kcal/oz), 18 g protein, 55 g carbohydrate, 5 g fiber, 2 g total sugars, 74 g fat

Net wt: 5.8 oz (including oil)   Exp. Date: _____

www.backcountryfoodie.com

To download this label template, visit

https://www.backcountryfoodie.com/labels/parmesan-pesto-ramen.pdf

or scan this barcode:

To find URL links for ingredients used, visit

https://backcountryfoodie.com/ingredients/

Garlic Parmesan Ramen

INGREDIENTS

1 package ramen noodles

1/4 cup parmesan cheese

1 1/2 Tbsp dried parsley

1/4 tsp garlic powder

1/4 tsp black pepper

1/8 tsp salt

4 Tbsp olive oil

Substitutions

Rice ramen noodles may be used as gluten-free alternative.

Shelf life will be extended if single serving packets of parmesan cheese are added at time of consumption or the meal is frozen until consumed.

AT HOME DIRECTIONS

1. Discard ramen noodle spice packet.
2. Put noodles in a bag or container to be used in the backcountry
3. Put remaining dry ingredients in a second bag to be stored inside the noodle bag.
4. Pack 4 Tbsp olive oil, per serving, in a leakproof container to be added to the meal when consumed. Recommend double bagging the oil in the event there is a leak

FIELD DIRECTIONS

1. Remove parmesan bag.
2. Add 8 oz hot/cold water or enough to cover noodles.
3. Let stand allowing noodles to rehydrate.
4. Consume or properly discard the noodle broth to practice the Leave No Trace principle.
5. Add parmesan packet and 4 Tbsp olive oil to noodles.
6. Stir and enjoy!

VEGETARIAN

GLUTEN-FREE OPTION

NUT-FREE

COOK

COLD SOAK

HOME PREP

Mix Dry Ingred.

HOME PREP TIME

5 Min

FIELD PREP

Cook, Cold Soak

FIELD PREP TIME

5-30 Min

TOTAL SERVINGS

1

WEIGHT/ SERVING

6.2 oz

	KCAL/OZ	CALORIES	PROTEIN	CARBS	FIBER	SUGAR	FAT
Nutrition Info PER SERVING	**158**	**982**	**21g**	**53g**	**3g**	**2g**	**78g**

35

Download the Label File for

Garlic Parmesan Ramen

Directions: Add 8 oz hot/cold water to cover noodles. Let stand to rehydrate. Consume or properly discard broth. Add dry ingredients packet and 4 Tbsp olive oil. Stir and enjoy!

Ingredients: ramen noodles, parmesan cheese, parsley, garlic powder, black pepper, salt

Nutrition: 982 kcal (158 kcal/oz), 21 g protein, 53 g carbohydrate, 3 g fiber, 2 g total sugars, 78 g fat

Net wt: 6.2 oz (including oil)   Exp. Date: _____

www.backcountryfoodie.com

To download this label template, visit

https://www.backcountryfoodie.com/labels/garlic-parmesan-ramen.pdf

or scan this barcode:

To find URL links for ingredients used, visit

https://backcountryfoodie.com/ingredients/

Carrot Salad

INGREDIENTS

1/4 cup dehydrated carrots, diced

1/8 cup freeze dried pineapple

1 Tbsp raisins

1 Tbsp brown sugar

1/2 packet True Lemon® powder

1/4 cup pecans

1 Tbsp coconut oil

AT HOME DIRECTIONS

1. Put all dry ingredients in bag or container to be used in the backcountry.

2. Pack 1 Tbsp (1 – 0.5 oz packet) coconut oil, per serving, in a leakproof container to be added to the meal when consumed. Recommend double bagging the oil in the event there is a leak

FIELD DIRECTIONS

1. Add 4 oz cold water or enough to cover the ingredients.

2. Stir and let stand 30-60 minutes allowing meal to rehydrate.

3. Warm coconut oil in your hands or sunlight encouraging it to liquify. This will allow the oil to mix with the carrots better.

4. Add 1 Tbsp (1 – 0.5 oz packet) coconut oil to the mix.

5. Stir and enjoy!

VEGAN

GLUTEN-FREE

COLD SOAK

HOME PREP
Mix Dry Ingred.

HOME PREP TIME
5 Min

FIELD PREP
Cold Soak

FIELD PREP TIME
30-60 Min

TOTAL SERVINGS
1

WEIGHT/ SERVING
3.1 oz

Nutrition Info PER SERVING	KCAL/OZ	CALORIES	PROTEIN	CARBS	FIBER	SUGAR	FAT
	153	475	4g	44g	8g	32g	33g

Download the Label File for

Carrot Salad

Directions: Add 4 oz water to bag. Stir and let stand for approximately 30-60 minutes. Add 1 Tbsp liquified coconut oil after rehydrated. Stir and enjoy!

Ingredients: carrots, pineapple, raisins, brown sugar, lemon powder, pecans

Nutrition: 475 kcal (153 kcal/oz), 4 g protein, 44 g carbohydrate, 8 g fiber, 32 g total sugars, 33 g fat

Net wt: 3.1 oz (including oil)   **Exp. Date:** _____

www.backcountryfoodie.com

To download this label template, visit

https://www.backcountryfoodie.com/labels/carrot-salad.pdf

or scan this barcode:

To find URL links for ingredients used, visit

https://backcountryfoodie.com/ingredients/

Thai Peanut Ramen

INGREDIENTS

1 package ramen noodles

1 Tbsp dehydrated carrots, diced

2 Tbsp coconut milk powder

1 Tbsp peanuts, chopped

1/2 tsp ginger

1/8-1/4 tsp red pepper flakes

1 packet True Lime® powder

2 Tbsp peanut butter

1 tbsp coconut oil

Substitutions

Rice ramen noodles may be used as gluten-free alternative.

AT HOME DIRECTIONS

1. Discard ramen noodle spice packet.

2. Put ramen noodles and carrots in a bag or container to be used in the backcountry.

3. Put the remaining dry ingredients in a separate bag to be stored with the noodles.

4. Pair with 2 Tbsp (1 – 1.15 oz packet) of peanut butter.

5. Pack 1 Tbsp (1 – 0.5 oz packet) coconut oil, per serving, in a leakproof container to be added to the meal when consumed. Recommend double bagging the oil in the event there is a leak

FIELD DIRECTIONS

1. Remove sauce packet.

2. Add 8 oz hot water to the noodle bag.

3. Let stand allowing noodles and carrots to rehydrate.

4. Consume or properly discard all but 2 oz of broth. Remaining

broth will be used to rehydrate the sauce.

5. Add the sauce packet, peanut butter and 1 Tbsp (1 - 0.5 oz packet) coconut oil to noodles.

6. Stir to mix well and enjoy!

VEGAN

GLUTEN-FREE OPTION

COOK

HOME PREP

Mix Dry Ingred.

HOME PREP TIME

3 Min

FIELD PREP

Cook

FIELD PREP TIME

5 Min

TOTAL SERVINGS

1

WEIGHT/ SERVING

5.7 oz

	KCAL/OZ	CALORIES	PROTEIN	CARBS	FIBER	SUGAR	FAT
Nutrition Info PER SERVING	148	846	22g	67g	8g	5g	57g

Download the Label File for

Thai Peanut Ramen

Directions: Add 8 oz hot water to cover noodles. Let stand until rehydrated. Consume or properly discard all but 2 oz broth. Add sauce packet, 2 Tbsp (1 packet) peanut butter and 1 Tbsp (1 packet) coconut oil. Stir well and enjoy!

Ingredients: ramen noodles, carrots, coconut milk powder, peanuts, ginger, red pepper flakes, lime powder, peanut butter

Nutrition: 846 kcal (148 kcal/oz), 22 g protein, 67 g carbohydrate, 8 g fiber, 5 g total sugars, 57 g fat

Net wt: 5.7 oz (including oil)   **Exp. Date:** _____

www.backcountryfoodie.com

To download this label template, visit

https://www.backcountryfoodie.com/labels/thai-peanut-ramen.pdf

or scan this barcode:

To find URL links for ingredients used, visit

https://backcountryfoodie.com/ingredients/

Lemon Parmesan Couscous

INGREDIENTS

1/2 cup couscous

2 Tbsp freeze-dried parmesan cheese

2 Tbsp pine nuts

1/8 cup freeze dried green bell peppers

1 tsp dried minced garlic

1 packet True Lemon® powder

1/4 tsp black pepper

2 Tbsp olive oil

AT HOME DIRECTIONS

1. Put all dry ingredients in bag or container to be used in the backcountry.

2. Pack 2 Tbsp olive oil, per serving, in a leakproof container to be added to the meal when consumed. Recommend double bagging the oil in the event there is a leak

FIELD DIRECTIONS

1. Add 6 oz hot water to bag.

2. Stir and let stand allowing the meal to rehydrate.

3. Add 2 Tbsp olive oil.

4. Stir and enjoy!

VEGETARIAN

COOK

HOME PREP
Mix Dry Ingred.

HOME PREP TIME
3 Min

FIELD PREP
Cook

FIELD PREP TIME
3 Min

TOTAL SERVINGS
1

WEIGHT/ SERVING
5.3 oz

Nutrition Info PER SERVING	KCAL/OZ	CALORIES	PROTEIN	CARBS	FIBER	SUGAR	FAT
	146	772	20g	74g	6g	2g	44g

Download the Label File for

Lemon Parmesan Couscous

Directions: Add 6 oz hot water and let stand to rehydrate. Add 2 Tbsp olive oil. Stir and enjoy!

Ingredients: couscous, freeze dried parmesan cheese, pine nuts, green bell peppers, minced garlic, lemon powder, black pepper

Nutrition: 772 kcal (146 kcal/oz), 20 g protein, 74 g carbohydrate, 6 g fiber, 2 g total sugars, 44 g fat

Net wt: 5.3 oz (including oil)   **Exp. Date:** _____

www.backcountryfoodie.com

To download this label template, visit

https://www.backcountryfoodie.com/labels/lemon-parmesan-couscous.pdf

or scan this barcode:

To find URL links for ingredients used, visit

https://backcountryfoodie.com/ingredients/

Beans and Cheese Fritos®

INGREDIENTS

2 oz bag Fritos® original corn chips

1/2 cup dehydrated instant refried beans

1/8 cup freeze dried cheddar cheese

2 tsp taco seasoning (or to taste)

1 Tbsp olive oil

AT HOME DIRECTIONS

1. Put all dry ingredients in a bag or container to be used in the backcountry.

2. Pair with 2 oz bag of Fritos® original corn chips.

3. Pack 1 Tbsp olive oil, per serving, in a leakproof container to be added to the meal when consumed. Recommend double bagging the oil in the event there is a leak

FIELD DIRECTIONS

1. Add 6 oz hot water to beans and cheese mix.

2. Stir and let stand allowing beans to rehydrate and cheese to melt.

3. Add 1 Tbsp olive oil to beans and cheese mix.

4. Stir, dip chips and enjoy!

VEGETARIAN

GLUTEN-FREE

NUT-FREE

COOK

HOME PREP
Mix Dry Ingred.

HOME PREP TIME
3 Min

FIELD PREP
Cook

FIELD PREP TIME
3 Min

TOTAL SERVINGS
1

WEIGHT/ SERVING
4.5 oz

	KCAL/OZ	CALORIES	PROTEIN	CARBS	FIBER	SUGAR	FAT
Nutrition Info PER SERVING	**146**	**658**	**22g**	**73g**	**16g**	**3g**	**43g**

Download the Label File for

Beans and Cheese Fritos®

Directions: Add 6 oz hot water or to desired consistency. Let stand. Add 1 Tbsp olive oil. Stir and enjoy!

Ingredients: Fritos® corn chips, refried beans, freeze-dried cheddar cheese, taco seasoning

Nutrition: 658 kcal (146 kcal/oz), 22 g protein, 73 g carbohydrate, 16 g fiber, 3 g total sugars, 43 g fat

Net wt: 4.5 oz (including oil)   **Exp. Date:** _____

www.backcountryfoodie.com

To download this label template, visit

https://www.backcountryfoodie.com/labels/beans-and-cheese-fritos.pdf

or scan this barcode:

To find URL links for ingredients used, visit

https://backcountryfoodie.com/ingredients/

Spicy Cashew Ramen

INGREDIENTS

1 package ramen noodles

1/4 cup freeze dried onion

1/2 tsp dried minced garlic

1/3 cup cashews, chopped

1 tsp dried parsley

1/4 tsp red chili pepper flakes

1/8 tsp salt

1 Tbsp olive oil

Substitution:

Rice ramen noodles may be used as gluten-free alternative.

AT HOME DIRECTIONS

1. Discard ramen noodle spice packet.

2. Put noodles, onion and garlic in a bag or container to be used in the backcountry.

3. Put remaining dry ingredients in a separate bag to be stored inside the noodle bag.

4. Pack 1 Tbsp olive oil, per serving, in a leakproof container to be added to the meal when consumed. Recommend double bagging the oil in the event there is a leak

FIELD DIRECTIONS

1. Remove dry ingredients packet.

2. Add 8 oz hot/cold water to noodle bag.

3. Let stand and allow noodles to rehydrate.

4. Consume or properly discard the noodle broth to practice the Leave No Trace principle. Meal may also be consumed as traditional ramen noodle soup.

5. Add dry ingredients packet and 1 Tbsp olive oil to noodles.

6. Stir and enjoy!

VEGAN

GLUTEN-FREE OPTION

COOK

COLD SOAK

HOME PREP

Mix Dry Ingred.

HOME PREP TIME

4 Min

FIELD PREP

Cook, Cold Soak

FIELD PREP TIME

5-30 Min

TOTAL SERVINGS

1

WEIGHT/ SERVING

5.3 oz

	KCAL/OZ	CALORIES	PROTEIN	CARBS	FIBER	SUGAR	FAT
Nutrition Info PER SERVING	144	765	16g	68g	4g	5g	50g

Download the Label File for

Spicy Cashew Ramen

Directions: Add 8 oz hot/cold water to cover noodles. Let stand until rehydrated. Consume or properly dischard broth. Add dry ingredients packet and 1 Tbsp olive oil. Stir and enjoy!

Ingredients: ramen noodles, onion, garlic, cashews, parsley, red pepper flakes, salt

Nutrition: 765 kcal (144 kcal/oz), 16 g protein, 68 g carbohydrate, 4 g fiber, 5 g total sugars, 50 g fat

Net wt: 5.3 oz (including oil)   Exp. Date: _____

www.backcountryfoodie.com

To download this label template, visit

https://www.backcountryfoodie.com/labels/spicy-cashew-ramen.pdf

or scan this barcode:

To find URL links for ingredients used, visit

https://backcountryfoodie.com/ingredients/

Chips & Salsa with Guacamole

INGREDIENTS

2 oz bag Fritos® original corn chips

Guacamole:

1 bag Alpine Aire® guacamole instant dip

1 packet True Lime® powder

1/8 tsp salt

Salsa:

1/4 cup sun-dried tomatoes, oil-free and chopped

1/8 cup freeze-dried onions

1 Tbsp tomato powder

2 packets True Lime® powder

1/2 tsp sugar

1/2 tsp dried minced garlic

1/2 tsp cilantro

1/8 tsp black pepper

1/8 tsp salt

1 Tbsp olive oil

AT HOME DIRECTIONS

1. Put all dry salsa ingredients directly into to the bag or container to be used in the backcountry.

2. Pair this with 2 oz bag of Fritos®, AlpineAire® guacamole mix and unopened packets of lime powder and salt.

3. Pack 1 Tbsp olive oil, per serving, in a leakproof container to be added to the meal when consumed. Recommend double bagging the oil in the event there is a leak.

FIELD DIRECTIONS

1. Add 3 oz cold water to salsa bag or to desired consistency.

2. Stir and let stand until rehydrated.

3. Once rehydrated, add 1 Tbsp olive oil and stir to mix well.

4. Add 2 oz cold water, lime powder and salt to guacamole bag.

5. Stir, dip chips and enjoy!

HOME PREP
Mix Dry Ingred.

HOME PREP TIME
10 Min

FIELD PREP
Cold Soak

FIELD PREP TIME
15-30 Min

TOTAL SERVINGS
1

WEIGHT/ SERVING
5.9 oz

Nutrition Info PER SERVING

	KCAL/OZ	CALORIES	PROTEIN	CARBS	FIBER	SUGAR	FAT
	144	851	13g	60g	12g	15g	68g

Download the Label File for

Chips & Salsa with Guacamole

Directions: Add 3 oz cold water to salsa. Stir and let stand. Add 1 Tbsp olive oil to salsa once rehdyrated. Add 2 oz cold water, lime packet and salt to guacamole. Stir, dip chips and enjoy!

Ingredients: corn chips, guacamole, lime powder, sun-dried tomatoes, onions, tomato powder, sugar, dried garlic, black pepper, cilantro, salt

Nutrition: 851 kcal (144 kcal/oz), 13 g protein, 60 g carbohydrate, 12 g fiber, 15 g total sugars, 68 g fat

Net wt: 5.9 oz (including oil)   Exp. Date: _____

www.backcountryfoodie.com

To download this label template, visit

https://www.backcountryfoodie.com/labels/chips-and-salsa-with-guacamole.pdf

or scan this barcode:

To find URL links for ingredients used, visit

https://backcountryfoodie.com/ingredients/

Parma Rosa Ramen

INGREDIENTS

1 package ramen noodles

1 Tbsp freeze dried red bell pepper

1 Tbsp freeze dried green onion

1 Tbsp freeze dried black olives, chopped

1 1/2 Tbsp Knorr® Parma Rosa sauce mix

2 Tbsp freeze dried parmesan cheese

1 Tbsp butter powder

1 Tbsp olive oil

Substitution:

Rice ramen noodles may be used as gluten-free alternative.

AT HOME DIRECTIONS

1. Discard ramen noodle spice packet.

2. Put noodles, peppers, onions and olives in a bag or container to be used in the backcountry.

3. Put remaining dry ingredients in a separate bag to be stored inside the noodle bag.

4. Pack 1 Tbsp olive oil, per serving, in a leakproof container to be added to the meal when consumed. Recommend double bagging the oil in the event there is a leak

FIELD DIRECTIONS

1. Remove sauce packet.

2. Add 8 oz hot water to noodle bag.

3. Let stand allowing noodles and vegetables to rehydrate.

4. Consume or properly discard all but 1 oz of the noodle broth to practice the Leave No Trace

principle. The remaining broth will be used to rehydrate the sauce mix.

5. Add sauce packet and stir well to evenly coat noodles.

6. Add 1 Tbsp olive oil.

7. Stir well and enjoy!

VEGETARIAN

GLUTEN-FREE OPTION

NUT-FREE

COOK

HOME PREP

Mix Dry Ingred.

HOME PREP TIME

3 Min

FIELD PREP

Cook

FIELD PREP TIME

5 Min

TOTAL SERVINGS

1

WEIGHT/ SERVING

4.7 oz

	KCAL/OZ	CALORIES	PROTEIN	CARBS	FIBER	SUGAR	FAT
Nutrition Info PER SERVING	**143**	**674**	**17g**	**60g**	**3g**	**5g**	**32g**

Download the Label File for

Parma Rosa Ramen

Directions: Remove sauce packet. Add 8 oz hot water to noodle bag and let stand. Consume or properly discard all but 1 oz of the broth. Add the sauce packet and 1 Tbsp olive oil. Stir and enjoy!

Ingredients: ramen noodles, red bell pepper, green onion, black olives, parma rosa dry sauce mix, parmesan cheese, butter powder

Nutrition: 674 kcal (143 kcal/oz), 17 g protein, 60 g carbohydrate, 3 g fiber, 5 g total sugars, 32 g fat

Net wt: 4.7 oz (including oil)   **Exp. Date:** _____

www.backcountryfoodie.com

To download this label template, visit

https://www.backcountryfoodie.com/labels/parma-rosa-ramen.pdf

or scan this barcode:

To find URL links for ingredients used, visit

https://backcountryfoodie.com/ingredients/

Italian Couscous

INGREDIENTS

1/2 cup couscous

1 Tbsp tomato powder

1/4 cup freeze dried parmesan cheese

1 tsp Italian seasoning

1/4 tsp black pepper

1/8 tsp salt

2 Tbsp olive oil

AT HOME DIRECTIONS

1. Put all dry ingredients in a bag or container to be used in the backcountry.

2. Pack 2 Tbsp olive oil, per serving, in a leakproof container to be added to the meal when consumed. Recommend double bagging the oil in the event there is a leak

FIELD DIRECTIONS

1. Add 6 oz hot water to bag.

2. Stir and let stand allowing the cheese to melt.

3. Add 2 Tbsp olive oil to bag.

4. Stir and enjoy!

HOME PREP
Mix Dry Ingred.

HOME PREP TIME
3 Min

FIELD PREP
Cook

FIELD PREP TIME
3 Min

TOTAL SERVINGS
1

WEIGHT/ SERVING
5.4 oz

	KCAL/OZ	CALORIES	PROTEIN	CARBS	FIBER	SUGAR	FAT
Nutrition Info PER SERVING	140	757	25g	75g	6g	5g	38g

Download the Label File for

Italian Couscous

Directions: Add 6 oz hot water or to desired consistency. Stir and let stand. Add 2 Tbsp olive oil. Stir and enjoy!

Ingredients: couscous, tomato powder, freeze dried parmesan cheese, italian seasoning, salt, pepper

Nutrition: 757 kcal (140 kcal/oz), 25 g protein, 75 g carbohydrate, 6 g fiber, 5 g total sugars, 38 g fat

Net wt: 5.4 oz (including oil)   Exp. Date: _____

www.backcountryfoodie.com

To download this label template, visit

https://www.backcountryfoodie.com/labels/italian-couscous.pdf

or scan this barcode:

To find URL links for ingredients used, visit

https://backcountryfoodie.com/ingredients/

Lemon Butter Ramen

INGREDIENTS

1 package ramen noodles

2 Tbsp parmesan cheese

1 1/2 Tbsp butter powder

1 packet True Lemon® powder

1/4 tsp black pepper

1 Tbsp olive oil

Substitutions

Rice ramen noodles may be used as gluten-free alternative.

Shelf life will be extended if single serving packets of parmesan cheese are added at time of consumption or the meal is frozen until consumed.

AT HOME DIRECTIONS

1. Discard ramen noodle spice packet.

2. Put noodles in a bag or container to be used in the backcountry.

3. Put remaining dry ingredients in a separate bag to be stored inside noodle bag.

4. Pack 1 Tbsp olive oil, per serving, in a leakproof container to be added to the meal when consumed. Recommend double bagging the oil in the event there is a leak

FIELD DIRECTIONS

1. Remove butter packet from noodle bag.

2. Add 8 oz of hot water to noodle bag.

3. Let stand allowing noodles to rehydrate.

4. Add 1 oz cold water to butter packet. Close packet and massage with fingertips to mix ingredients well.

5. Consume or properly discard all but 1 oz noodle broth to practice the Leave No Trace principle. Remaining broth will be used to fully rehydrate butter sauce.

6. Add contents of butter packet and stir well to evenly coat noodles.

7. Add 1 Tbsp olive oil.

8. Stir and enjoy!

VEGETARIAN

GLUTEN-FREE OPTION

NUT-FREE

COOK

HOME PREP

Mix Dry Ingred.

HOME PREP TIME

3 Min

FIELD PREP

Cook

FIELD PREP TIME

5 Min

TOTAL SERVINGS

1

WEIGHT/ SERVING

4.4 oz

Nutrition Info PER SERVING	KCAL/OZ	CALORIES	PROTEIN	CARBS	FIBER	SUGAR	FAT
	140	615	16g	53g	3g	3g	38g

Download the Label File for

Lemon Butter Ramen

Directions: Add 8 oz hot water to noodles and let stand. Add 1 oz cold water to butter packet, close packet and massage with fingers. Consume or properly discard all but 1 oz of broth. Add butter mixture and 1 Tbsp olive oil to noodles. Stir and enjoy!

Ingredients: ramen noodles, parmesan cheese, butter powder, lemon powder, black pepper

Nutrition: 615 kcal (140 kcal/oz), 16 g protein, 53 g carbohydrate, 3 g fiber, 3 g total sugars, 38 g fat

Net wt: 4.4 oz (including oil)   **Exp. Date:** _____

www.backcountryfoodie.com

To download this label template, visit

https://www.backcountryfoodie.com/labels/lemon-butter-ramen.pdf

or scan this barcode:

To find URL links for ingredients used, visit

https://backcountryfoodie.com/ingredients/

Sun-Dried Tomato Couscous

INGREDIENTS

1/2 cup couscous

3 pieces sun-dried tomatoes, oil-free and chopped

2 Tbsp pine nuts

1/2 tsp parsley

1/2 tsp oregano

1/2 tsp basil

1/2 tsp turmeric

1/2 tsp garlic powder

1/4 tsp black pepper

1/4 tsp salt

2 Tbsp olive oil

Note:

Avoid using sun-dried tomatoes stored in oil as this will increase the risk of rancidity.

AT HOME DIRECTIONS

1. Put all dry ingredients into a bag or container to be used in the backcountry.

2. Pack 2 Tbsp olive oil, per serving, in a leakproof container to be added to the meal when consumed. Recommend double bagging the oil in the event there is a leak

FIELD DIRECTIONS

1. Add 6 oz hot/cold water and let stand until rehydrated.

2. Add 2 Tbsp olive oil.

3. Stir and enjoy!

VEGAN

COOK

COLD SOAK

HOME PREP

Mix Dry Ingred.

HOME PREP TIME

3 Min

FIELD PREP

Cook, Cold Soak

FIELD PREP TIME

3-20 Min

TOTAL SERVINGS

1

WEIGHT/ SERVING

5.5 oz

Nutrition Info PER SERVING	KCAL/OZ	CALORIES	PROTEIN	CARBS	FIBER	SUGAR	FAT
	140	770	17g	81g	10g	7g	42g

Download the Label File for

Sun-Dried Tomato Couscous

Directions: Add 6 oz hot/cold water or to desired consistency. Stir and let stand. Add 2 Tbsp olive oil. Stir and enjoy!

Ingredients: couscous, sun-dried tomatoes, pine nuts, parsley, oregano, basil, turmeric, garlic powder, salt, pepper

Nutrition: 770 kcal (140 kcal/oz), 17 g protein, 81 g carbohydrate, 10 g fiber, 7 g total sugars, 42 g fat

Net wt: 5.5 oz (including oil)   Exp. Date: _____

www.backcountryfoodie.com

To download this label template, visit

https://www.backcountryfoodie.com/labels/sun-dried-tomato-couscous.pdf

or scan this barcode:

To find URL links for ingredients used, visit

https://backcountryfoodie.com/ingredients/

Trail Tabbouleh

INGREDIENTS

1/2 cup bulgur

1/4 cup freeze dried onion

4 pieces sun dried tomatoes, oil-free and chopped

2 Tbsp dried parsley

2 tsp dried mint leaves

2 packets True Lemon® powder

1/2 tsp salt

1/2 tsp black pepper

3 Tbsp olive oil

AT HOME DIRECTIONS

1. Put all dry ingredients in a bag or container to be used in the backcountry.

2. Pack 3 Tbsp olive oil, per serving, in a leakproof container to be added to the meal when consumed. Recommend double bagging the oil in the event there is a leak

FIELD DIRECTIONS

1. Add 6 oz cold water to bag.

2. Stir and let stand allowing the meal to rehydrate. Add more water as needed to meet desired consistency.

3. Add 3 Tbsp olive oil.

4. Stir and enjoy!

VEGAN

GLUTEN-FREE

NUT-FREE

COLD SOAK

HOME PREP
Mix Dry Ingred.

HOME PREP TIME
5 Min

FIELD PREP
Cold Soak

FIELD PREP TIME
60 Min

TOTAL SERVINGS
1

WEIGHT/ SERVING
5.2 oz

	KCAL/OZ	CALORIES	PROTEIN	CARBS	FIBER	SUGAR	FAT
Nutrition Info PER SERVING	139	723	12g	76g	12g	7g	42g

Download the Label File for

Trail Tabbouleh

Directions: Add 6 oz cold water. Stir and let stand to rehydrate for approximately 60 minutes. Add 3 Tbsp olive oil. Stir and enjoy!

Ingredients: bulgur, onion, sun dried tomatoes, parsley, mint, lemon powder, salt, black pepper

Nutrition: 723 kcal (139 kcal/oz), 12 g protein, 76 g carbohydrate, 12 g fiber, 7 g total sugars, 42 g fat

Net wt: 5.2 oz (including oil)   Exp. Date: _____

www.backcountryfoodie.com

To download this label template, visit

https://www.backcountryfoodie.com/labels/trail-tabbouleh.pdf

or scan this barcode:

To find URL links for ingredients used, visit

https://backcountryfoodie.com/ingredients/

Zucchini And Pecan Salad

INGREDIENTS

1/2 cup freeze dried zucchini

1/2 cup freeze dried apple

2 Tbsp pecans, chopped

1 packet True Lemon® powder

1 Tbsp sugar

1/4 tsp ginger, ground

1/2 Tbsp olive oil

AT HOME DIRECTIONS

1. Put all dry ingredients in a bag or container to be used in the backcountry.

2. Pack 1/2 Tbsp olive oil, per serving, in a leakproof container to be added to the meal when consumed. Recommend double bagging the oil in the event there is a leak

FIELD DIRECTIONS

1. Add 4 oz cold water or enough to cover the contents of the bag.

2. Stir and let stand allowing the meal to rehydrate.

3. Add ½ Tbsp olive oil.

4. Stir and enjoy!

Note: This is a low calorie but moderate volume meal. Recommend pairing with another side dish such as a spread and crackers, dessert or nut mix.

VEGAN

GLUTEN-FREE

COLD SOAK

HOME PREP

Mix Dry Ingred.

HOME PREP TIME

5 Min

FIELD PREP

Cold Soak

FIELD PREP TIME

20 Min

TOTAL SERVINGS

1

WEIGHT/ SERVING

1.9 oz

Nutrition Info PER SERVING

KCAL/OZ	CALORIES	PROTEIN	CARBS	FIBER	SUGAR	FAT
138	262	2g	29g	2g	23g	17g

Download the Label File for

Zucchini & Pecan Salad

Directions: Add 4 oz cold water or enough to cover the contents of the bag. Stir and let stand to rehydrate. Add 1/2 Tbsp olive oil. Stir and enjoy!

Ingredients: zucchini, apples, pecans, lemon powder, sugar, ginger

Nutrition: 262 kcal (138 kcal/oz), 2 g protein, 29 g carbohydrate, 2 g fiber, 23 g total sugars, 17 g fat

Net wt: 1.9 oz (including oil)   **Exp. Date:** _____

www.backcountryfoodie.com

To download this label template, visit

https://www.backcountryfoodie.com/labels/zucchini-salad.pdf

or scan this barcode:

To find URL links for ingredients used, visit

https://backcountryfoodie.com/ingredients/

Pineapple & Peppers Couscous

INGREDIENTS

1/2 cup couscous

2 Tbsp freeze dried green bell peppers

1 Tbsp freeze dried onion

3 Tbsp freeze dried pineapple

1 packet True Lime® powder

2 Tbsp cashews, chopped

1/4 tsp black pepper

2 Tbsp olive oil

AT HOME DIRECTIONS

1. Put all ingredients in a bag or container to be used in the backcountry.

2. Pack 2 Tbsp olive oil, per serving, in a leakproof container to be added to the meal when consumed. Recommend double bagging the oil in the event there is a leak

FIELD DIRECTIONS

1. Add 6 oz hot/cold water to bag.

2. Stir and let stand allowing meal to rehydrate.

3. Add 2 Tbsp olive oil.

4. Stir and enjoy!

VEGAN

COOK

COLD SOAK

HOME PREP

Mix Dry Ingred.

HOME PREP TIME

4 Min

FIELD PREP

Cook, Cold Soak

FIELD PREP TIME

3-20 Min

TOTAL SERVINGS

1

WEIGHT/ SERVING

5.0 oz

	KCAL/OZ	CALORIES	PROTEIN	CARBS	FIBER	SUGAR	FAT
Nutrition Info PER SERVING	138	690	14g	80g	6g	6g	36g

Download the Label File for

Pineapple & Peppers Couscous

Directions: Add 6 oz hot/cold water or to desired consistency. Stir and let stand. Add 2 Tbsp olive oil. Stir and enjoy!

Ingredients: couscous, green pepper, onion, pineapple, lime powder, cashews, black pepper

Nutrition: 690 kcal (138 kcal/oz), 14 g protein, 80 g carbohydrate, 6 g fiber, 6 g total sugars, 36 g fat

Net wt: 5 oz (including oil)   **Exp. Date:** _____

www.backcountryfoodie.com

To download this label template, visit

https://www.backcountryfoodie.com/labels/pineapple-and-peppers-couscous.pdf

or scan this barcode:

To find URL links for ingredients used, visit

https://backcountryfoodie.com/ingredients/

Backcountry Spaghetti

INGREDIENTS

1 package ramen noodles

1/8 cup freeze dried onion

1/8 cup freeze dried mushrooms

1/8 cup tomato powder

1/8 cup freeze dried parmesan cheese

1/2 tsp Italian seasoning

1/4 tsp sugar

1/4 tsp garlic powder

1/8 tsp salt

1/8 tsp black pepper

1 Tbsp olive oil

Substitutions

Rice ramen noodles may be used as gluten-free alternative.

AT HOME DIRECTIONS

1. Discard ramen noodle spice packet.

2. Put noodles, onions and mushrooms in a bag or container to be used in the backcountry.

3. Put remaining dry ingredients in a separate bag to be stored inside the noodle bag.

4. Pack 1 Tbsp olive oil, per serving, in a leakproof container to be added to the meal when consumed. Recommend double bagging the oil in the event there is a leak

FIELD DIRECTIONS

1. Remove sauce packet.

2. Add 8 oz hot water to noodle bag.

3. Let stand allowing noodles to rehydrate.

4. Consume or properly discard all but 2 oz of noodle broth to practice the Leave No Trace principle. Remaining broth to be used to rehydrate sauce mix.

5. Add sauce packet to noodles and stir well.

6. Cheese melts best if meal is kept hot using an insulated cozy or putting the meal (double bagged) in your puffy jacket pocket.

7. Once mixed well, add 1 Tbsp olive oil.

8. Stir and enjoy!

GLUTEN-FREE OPTION

NUT-FREE

COOK

HOME PREP

Mix Dry Ingred.

HOME PREP TIME

4 Min

FIELD PREP

Cook

FIELD PREP TIME

7 Min

TOTAL SERVINGS

1

WEIGHT/ SERVING

4.6 oz

Nutrition Info PER SERVING	KCAL/OZ	CALORIES	PROTEIN	CARBS	FIBER	SUGAR	FAT
	137	630	17g	65g	5g	10g	34g

Download the Label File for

Backcountry Spaghetti

Directions: Remove sauce packet. Add 8 oz hot water to cover noodles. Let stand until rehydrated. Consume or properly discard all but 2 oz of the broth. Add sauce packet and 1 Tbsp olive oil. Stir well and enjoy!

Ingredients: ramen noodles, tomato powder, freeze dried parmesan cheese, onion, mushrooms, italian seasoning, sugar, garlic powder, salt, black pepper

Nutrition: 630 kcal (137 kcal/oz), 17 g protein, 65 g carbohydrate, 5 g fiber, 10 g total sugars, 34 g fat

Net wt: 4.6 oz (including oil)   **Exp. Date:** _____

www.backcountryfoodie.com

To download this label template, visit

https://www.backcountryfoodie.com/labels/backcountry-spaghetti.pdf

or scan this barcode:

To find URL links for ingredients used, visit

https://backcountryfoodie.com/ingredients/

Lemon Pepper Bean Spread

INGREDIENTS

1/2 cup dehydrated instant refried beans

1/8 cup freeze dried onions

1 Tbsp sesame seeds

1 1/2 tsp lemon pepper seasoning

1/8 tsp garlic powder

1/4 tsp onion powder

1/8 tsp cumin, ground

2 Tbsp olive oil

10 Trisuit® crackers, original flavor

Substitution:

Gluten-free crackers may be used as a gluten-free alternative.

AT HOME DIRECTIONS

1. Put all dry ingredients, except crackers, in a bag or container to be used in the backcountry.

2. Pack 10 crackers to be paired with bean spread.

3. Pack 2 Tbsp olive oil, per serving, in a leakproof container to be added to the meal when consumed. Recommend double bagging the oil in the event there is a leak

FIELD DIRECTIONS

1. Add 6 oz hot/cold water to bag.

2. Stir and let stand allowing beans to rehydrate.

3. Add 2 Tbsp olive oil.

4. Stir to mix well, spread on crackers and enjoy!

VEGAN

GLUTEN-FREE OPTION

NUT-FREE

COOK

COLD SOAK

HOME PREP
Mix Dry Ingred.

HOME PREP TIME
3 Min

FIELD PREP
Cook, Cold Soak

FIELD PREP TIME
5-30 Min

TOTAL SERVINGS
1

WEIGHT/ SERVING
4.6 oz

	KCAL/OZ	CALORIES	PROTEIN	CARBS	FIBER	SUGAR	FAT
Nutrition Info PER SERVING	135	622	15g	64g	16g	<1g	35g

Download the Label File for

Lemon Pepper Bean Spread

Directions: Add 6 oz hot/cold water or to desired consistency. Let stand to rehydrate. Add 2 Tbsp olive oil. Stir and enjoy! Pair with 10 Triscuit® crackers.

Ingredients: instant dehydrated refried beans, sesame seeds, onion, lemon pepper seasoning, garlic powder, onion powder, cumin

Nutrition: 622 kcal (135 kcal/oz), 15 g protein, 64 g carbohydrate, 16 g fiber, <1 g total sugars, 35 g fat

Net wt: 4.6 oz (including oil)   Exp. Date: _____

www.backcountryfoodie.com

To download this label template, visit

https://www.backcountryfoodie.com/labels/lemon-pepper-bean-spread.pdf

or scan this barcode:

To find URL links for ingredients used, visit

https://backcountryfoodie.com/ingredients/

Tex-Mex Ramen

INGREDIENTS

1 package ramen noodles

1 Tbsp freeze dried onions

1 Tbsp freeze dried green onions

1/4 cup dehydrated instant refried beans

1/4 cup freeze dried cheddar cheese

2 tsp taco seasoning

1 Tbsp olive oil

AT HOME DIRECTIONS

1. Discard ramen noodle spice packet.

2. Put noodles, onions and green onions in a bag or storage container to be used in the backcountry.

3. Put beans, cheese and taco seasoning in separate bag to be stored inside the noodle bag.

4. Pack 1 Tbsp olive oil, per serving, in a leakproof container to be added to the meal when consumed. Recommend double bagging the oil in the event there is a leak

FIELD DIRECTIONS

1. Remove the beans and cheese packet.

2. Add 8 oz hot water to noodles.

3. Let stand allowing noodles to rehydrate.

4. Add 4 oz hot water to beans and cheese.

5. Stir and let stand allowing beans to rehydrate and cheese to melt.

6. Once rehydrated, consume or properly discard noodle broth to practice the Leave No Trace principle.

7. Add beans and cheese mix to noodles.

8. Stir to mix well.

9. Add 1 Tbsp olive oil.

10. Stir and enjoy!

VEGETARIAN

NUT-FREE

COOK

HOME PREP
Mix Dry Ingred.

HOME PREP TIME
4 Min

FIELD PREP
Cook

FIELD PREP TIME
6 Min

TOTAL SERVINGS
1

WEIGHT/ SERVING
5.2 oz

	KCAL/OZ	CALORIES	PROTEIN	CARBS	FIBER	SUGAR	FAT
Nutrition Info PER SERVING	135	702	21g	69g	7g	3g	38g

Download the Label File for

Tex-Mex Ramen

Directions: Add 8 oz hot water to noodle bag and 4 oz hot water to beans packet. Let stand allowing both to redhyrate. Consume or properly discard the broth once rehydrated. Add beans and 1 Tbsp olive oil to noodles. Stir and enjoy!

Ingredients: ramen noodles, dehydrated refried beans, freeze dried cheddar cheese, onion, green onion, taco seasoning

Nutrition: 702 kcal (135 kcal/oz), 21 g protein, 69 g carbohydrate, 7 g fiber, 3 g total sugars, 38 g fat

Net wt: 5.2 oz (including oil)   **Exp. Date:** _____

www.backcountryfoodie.com

To download this label template, visit

https://www.backcountryfoodie.com/labels/tex-mex-ramen.pdf

or scan this barcode:

To find URL links for ingredients used, visit

https://backcountryfoodie.com/ingredients/

Apricot Rosemary Couscous

INGREDIENTS

1/2 cup couscous

1/8 cup dried apricots, chopped

2 Tbsp pecans, chopped

1 tsp dried rosemary

1 tsp dried minced garlic

1/4 tsp black pepper

1/8 tsp salt

2 Tbsp olive oil

AT HOME DIRECTIONS

1. Put all dry ingredients in a bag or container to be used in the backcountry.

2. Pack 2 Tbsp olive oil, per serving, in a leakproof container to be added to the meal when consumed. Recommend double bagging the oil in the event there is a leak

FIELD DIRECTIONS

1. Add 6 oz hot/cold water to bag.

2. Stir and let stand allowing the meal to rehydrate.

3. Add 2 Tbsp olive oil.

4. Stir and enjoy!

VEGAN

COOK

COLD SOAK

HOME PREP

Mix Dry Ingred.

HOME PREP TIME

4 Min

FIELD PREP

Cook, Cold Soak

FIELD PREP TIME

3-15 Min

TOTAL SERVINGS

1

WEIGHT/ SERVING

5.4 oz

	KCAL/OZ	CALORIES	PROTEIN	CARBS	FIBER	SUGAR	FAT
Nutrition Info PER SERVING	**134**	**722**	**13g**	**85g**	**8g**	**12g**	**38g**

69

Download the Label File for

Apricot Rosemary Couscous

Directions: Add 6 oz hot/cold water or to desired consistency. Let stand. Add 2 Tbsp olive oil. Stir and enjoy!

Ingredients: couscous, apricots, pecans, rosemary, garlic, black pepper, salt

Nutrition: 722 kcal (134 kcal/oz), 13 g protein, 85 g carbohydrate, 8 g fiber, 12 g total sugars, 38 g fat

Net wt: 5.4 oz (including oil)   Exp. Date: _____

www.backcountryfoodie.com

To download this label template, visit

https://www.backcountryfoodie.com/labels/apricot-rosemary-couscous.pdf

or scan this barcode:

To find URL links for ingredients used, visit

https://backcountryfoodie.com/ingredients/

Spicy Mushroom & Onion Ramen

INGREDIENTS

1 package ramen noodles

1/8 cup freeze dried onions

1/8 cup freeze dried mushrooms

1 Tbsp dried chives

1/8 cup textured vegetable protein (TVP)

1/8 tsp red pepper flakes

1/8 tsp ginger, ground

1/8 tsp black pepper

dash salt

1 Tbsp olive oil

Substitutions

Rice ramen noodles may be used as gluten-free alternative.

AT HOME DIRECTIONS

1. Discard ramen noodle spice packet.

2. Put all dry ingredients in a bag or container to be used in the backcountry.

3. Pack 1 Tbsp olive oil, per serving, in a leakproof container to be added to the meal when consumed. Recommend double bagging the oil in the event there is a leak

FIELD DIRECTIONS

1. Add 8 oz hot/cold water to bag.

2. Let stand allowing the meal to rehydrate.

3. Recipe is intended to be consumed as traditional ramen noodle soup. Consume broth to practice the Leave No Trace principle.

4. Add 1 Tbsp olive oil.

5. Stir and enjoy!

VEGAN

GLUTEN-FREE OPTION

NUT-FREE

COOK

COLD SOAK

HOME PREP

Mix Dry Ingred.

HOME PREP TIME

3 Min

FIELD PREP

Cook, Cold Soak

FIELD PREP TIME

5-60 Min

TOTAL SERVINGS

1

WEIGHT/ SERVING

4.1 oz

Nutrition nfo PER SERVING

KCAL/OZ	CALORIES	PROTEIN	CARBS	FIBER	SUGAR	FAT
134	549	15g	58g	5g	4g	29g

Download the Label File for

Spicy Mushroom & Onion Ramen

Directions: Add 8 oz hot/cold water. Let stand allowing meal to rehydrate. Meal to be consumed as traditional noodle soup. Add 1 Tbsp olive oil. Stir and enjoy!

Ingredients: ramen noodles, onion, mushroom, textured vegetable protein (TVP), red pepper flakes, ginger, chives, black pepper, salt,

Nutrition: 549 kcal (134 kcal/oz), 15 g protein, 58 g carbohydrate, 5 g fiber, 4 g total sugars, 29 g fat

Net wt: 4.1 oz (including oil)   **Exp. Date:** _____

www.backcountryfoodie.com

To download this label template, visit

https://www.backcountryfoodie.com/labels/spicy-mushroom-and-onion-ramen.pdf

or scan this barcode:

To find URL links for ingredients used, visit

https://backcountryfoodie.com/ingredients/

Vegetarian Stroganoff

INGREDIENTS

1 cup thin egg noodles, flat

1/4 cup freeze dried onion

1/4 cup freeze dried mushrooms

1/8 cup textured vegetable protein (TVP)

5 Tbsp sour cream powder

2 Tbsp butter powder

1/4 tsp black pepper

1/8 tsp salt

1/2 Tbsp olive oil

Substitution:

Gluten-free egg noodles may be used as gluten-free alternative.

AT HOME DIRECTIONS

1. Put all dry ingredients in a bag or container to be used in the backcountry.
2. Pack 1/2 Tbsp olive oil, per serving, in a leakproof container to be added to the meal when consumed. Recommend double bagging the oil in the event there is a leak

FIELD DIRECTIONS

1. Add 6 oz hot water to bag.
2. Stir and let stand allowing the meal to rehydrate. Note: Noodles cook faster if kept hot. Consider using an insulated cozy or double bagging the meal and putting it in your puffy jacket pocket.
3. Add ½ Tbsp olive oil.
4. Stir and enjoy!

HOME PREP

Mix Dry Ingred.

HOME PREP TIME

4 Min

FIELD PREP

Cook

FIELD PREP TIME

7 Min

TOTAL SERVINGS

1

WEIGHT/ SERVING

4.2 oz

	KCAL/OZ	CALORIES	PROTEIN	CARBS	FIBER	SUGAR	FAT
Nutrition nfo PER SERVING	**128**	**539**	**13g**	**59g**	**2g**	**15g**	**30g**

Download the Label File for

Vegetarian Stroganoff

Directions: Add 6 oz hot water or to desired consistency. Stir and let stand. Noodles cook best if bag/pot is insulated. Add 1/2 Tbsp olive oil after redhydrated. Stir and enjoy!

Ingredients: egg noodles, onion, mushroom, textured vegetable protein (TVP), sour cream powder, butter powder, black pepper, salt

Nutrition: 539 kcal (128 kcal/oz), 13 g protein, 59 g carbohydrate, 2 g fiber, 15 g total sugars, 30 g fat

Net wt: 4.2 oz (including oil)   Exp. Date: _____

www.backcountryfoodie.com

To download this label template, visit

https://www.backcountryfoodie.com/labels/vegetarian-stroganoff.pdf

or scan this barcode:

To find URL links for ingredients used, visit

https://backcountryfoodie.com/ingredients/

Garden Marinara Couscous

INGREDIENTS

1/2 cup couscous

1 Tbsp freeze dried mushrooms

1 Tbsp freeze dried onions

1 Tbsp freeze dried red bell peppers

1 Tbsp freeze dried green bell peppers

1 1/2 Tbsp tomato powder

1 Tbsp freeze dried parmesan cheese

1 Tbsp pine nuts

1 1/2 tsp dried minced garlic

1 tsp brown sugar

2 tsp Italian seasoning

1/4 tsp black pepper

1/8-1/4 tsp red chili pepper flakes

dash of salt

1 Tbsp olive oil

AT HOME DIRECTIONS

1. Put all dry ingredients in a bag or container to be used in the backcountry.
2. Pack 1 Tbsp olive oil, per serving, in a leakproof container to be added to the meal when consumed. Recommend double bagging the oil in the event there is a leak

FIELD DIRECTIONS

1. Add 8 oz hot water or to desired consistency.
2. Stir and let stand allowing meal to rehydrate.
3. Add 1 tbsp olive oil.
4. Stir and enjoy!

VEGETARIAN

COOK

HOME PREP

Mix Dry Ingred.

HOME PREP TIME

5 Min

FIELD PREP

Cook

FIELD PREP TIME

3 Min

TOTAL SERVINGS

1

WEIGHT/ SERVING

5.2 oz

Nutrition Info PER SERVING	KCAL/OZ	CALORIES	PROTEIN	CARBS	FIBER	SUGAR	FAT
	126	653	21g	86g	8g	11g	25g

Download the Label File for

Garden Marinara Couscous

Directions: Add 8 oz hot water and allow to rehydrate. Add 1 Tbsp olive oil. Stir and enjoy!

Ingredients: couscous, mushroom, onion, red bell pepper, green bell pepper, freeze dried parmesan cheese, tomato powder, pine nuts, garlic, Italian seasoning, red chilli pepper flakes, brown sugar, salt, black pepper

Nutrition: 653 kcal (126 kcal/oz), 21 g protein, 86 g carbohydrate, 8 g fiber, 11 g total sugars, 25 g fat

Net wt: 5.2 oz (including oil)   Exp. Date: _____

www.backcountryfoodie.com

To download this label template, visit

https://www.backcountryfoodie.com/labels/garden-marinara-couscous.pdf

or scan this barcode:

To find URL links for ingredients used, visit

https://backcountryfoodie.com/ingredients/

Herb & Cheese Spread with Crackers

INGREDIENTS

1/4 cup parmesan cheese powder

1/2 tsp garlic powder

1 Tbsp Italian seasoning

1 tsp olive oil

10 Triscuit® crackers, original flavor

Substitution:

Replace Triscuits with gluten-free crackers for a gluten-free alternative.

AT HOME DIRECTIONS

1. Put all dry ingredients, except crackers, in a bag or container to be used in the backcountry.
2. Pack 10 crackers per serving.
3. Pack 1 tsp olive oil, per serving, in a leakproof container to be added to the meal when consumed. Recommend double bagging the oil in the event there is a leak

FIELD DIRECTIONS

1. Add 1 Tbsp cold water and stir well.
2. Let stand allowing cheese spread to rehydrate. Slowly add more water as desired. Be aware that consistency will quickly become too thin.
3. Add 1 tsp olive oil.
4. Stir to mix well, spread on crackers and enjoy!

Note: Recommend doubling the portion for a hungry hiker or pairing with a side dish, dessert or nut mix.

VEGETARIAN

GLUTEN-FREE OPTION

NUT-FREE

NO-COOK

HOME PREP
Mix Dry Ingred.

HOME PREP TIME
3 Min

FIELD PREP
No Cook

FIELD PREP TIME
5 Min

TOTAL SERVINGS
1

WEIGHT/ SERVING
2.9 oz

Nutrition Info PER SERVING	KCAL/OZ	CALORIES	PROTEIN	CARBS	FIBER	SUGAR	FAT
	126	365	17g	35g	5g	<1g	18g

Download the Label File for

Herb & Cheese Spread with Crackers

Directions: Add 1 Tbsp cold water or to desired consistency. Stir well until spread thickens. Add 1 tsp olive oil. Stir, spread on crackers and enjoy!

Ingredients: parmesan cheese powder, garlic, Italian seasoning, Triscuit® original flavor crackers

Nutrition: 365 kcal (126 kcal/oz), 17 g protein, 35 g carbohydrate, 5 g fiber, <1 g total sugars, 18 g fat

Net wt: 2.9 oz (includes oil & crackers)   **Exp. Date:** _____

www.backcountryfoodie.com

To download this label template, visit

https://www.backcountryfoodie.com/labels/herb-and-cheese-spread-with-crackers.pdf

or scan this barcode:

To find URL links for ingredients used, visit

https://backcountryfoodie.com/ingredients/

Sweet & Savory Couscous

INGREDIENTS

1/2 cup couscous

2 Tbsp dried cherries, chopped

2 Tbsp raisins

2 Tbsp dehydrated carrots, diced

2 Tbsp dehydrated onion, minced

1/4 cup almonds, sliced

1 tsp vegetable bouillon powder

1 tsp garlic powder

1/2 tsp brown sugar

1 1/2 tsp chili powder

2 Tbsp olive oil

AT HOME DIRECTIONS

1. Put all dry ingredients in a bag or container to be used in the backcountry.
2. Pack 2 Tbsp olive oil, per serving, in a leakproof container to be added to the meal when consumed. Recommend double bagging the oil in the event there is a leak

FIELD DIRECTIONS

1. Add 6 oz hot/cold water to bag.
2. Stir and let stand allowing the meal to rehydrate.
3. Add 2 Tbsp olive oil.
4. Stir and enjoy!

HOME PREP

Mix Dry Ingred.

HOME PREP TIME

3 Min

FIELD PREP

Cook, Cold Soak

FIELD PREP TIME

3-10 Min

TOTAL SERVINGS

1

WEIGHT/ SERVING

7.3 oz

Nutrition Info PER SERVING	KCAL/OZ	CALORIES	PROTEIN	CARBS	FIBER	SUGAR	FAT
	125	**914**	**20g**	**122g**	**13g**	**29g**	**41g**

Download the Label File for

Sweet & Savory Couscous

Directions: Add 6 oz hot/cold water or to desired consistency. Stir and let stand. Add 2 Tbsp olive oil. Stir and enjoy!

Ingredients: couscous, cherries, raisins, carrots, onions, almonds, vegetable bouillon, chili powder, garlic, brown sugar

Nutrition: 914 kcal (125 kcal/oz), 20 g protein, 122 g carbohydrate, 13 g fiber, 29 g total sugars, 41 g fat

Net wt: 7.3 oz (including oil)   **Exp. Date:** _____

www.backcountryfoodie.com

To download this label template, visit

https://www.backcountryfoodie.com/labels/sweet-and-savory-couscous.pdf

or scan this barcode:

To find URL links for ingredients used, visit

https://backcountryfoodie.com/ingredients/

Vegetarian Burrito

INGREDIENTS

1/2 cup taco flavored textured vegetable protein (TVP)

1/2 cup dehydrated instant refried beans

1/4 cup freeze dried cheddar cheese

1 Tbsp olive oil

AT HOME DIRECTIONS

1. Put all dry ingredients in a bag or container to be used in the backcountry.

2. Pack 1 Tbsp olive oil, per serving, in a leakproof container to be added to the meal when consumed. Recommend double bagging the oil in the event there is a leak

FIELD DIRECTIONS

1. Add 8 oz hot water to bag.

2. Stir and let stand allowing the beans and cheese to melt.

3. Add 1 Tbsp olive oil.

4. Stir, spread on tortilla or eat as is and enjoy!

HOME PREP

Mix Dry Ingred.

HOME PREP TIME

3 Min

FIELD PREP

Cook

FIELD PREP TIME

5 Min

TOTAL SERVINGS

1

WEIGHT/ SERVING

5.0 oz

Nutrition Info PER SERVING	KCAL/OZ	CALORIES	PROTEIN	CARBS	FIBER	SUGAR	FAT
	123	614	42g	47g	19g	5g	29g

Download the Label File for

Vegetarian Burrito

Directions: Add 8 oz hot water and let stand to rehydrate. Add 1 Tbsp olive oil. Stir and enjoy!

Ingredients: instant dehydrated refried beans, taco flavored textured vegetable protein (TVP), cheddar cheese

Nutrition: 614 kcal (123 kcal/oz), 42 g protein, 47 g carbohydrate, 19 g fiber, 5 g total sugars, 29 g fat

Net wt: 5 oz (including oil)   **Exp. Date:** _____

www.backcountryfoodie.com

To download this label template, visit

https://www.backcountryfoodie.com/labels/vegetarian-burrito.pdf

or scan this barcode:

To find URL links for ingredients used, visit

https://backcountryfoodie.com/ingredients/

SNACKS

Chocolate Almond Butter Snack

INGREDIENTS

1/4 cup old fashioned oats

1/8 cup oat bran

1/8 cup dark chocolate chips

2 tsp honey crystals

1/4 cup almond butter

1 Tbsp coconut oil

Substitutions

Use carob chips as a vegan alternative option. Various nut butters may also be used.

AT HOME DIRECTIONS

1. Put all dry ingredients in a bag or container to be used in the backcountry.

2. Pair with 1/4 cup (2 - 1.1 oz packets) almond butter.

3. Pack 1 Tbsp (1 – 0.5 oz packet) coconut oil, per serving, in a leakproof container to be added to the meal when consumed. Recommend double bagging the oil in the event there is a leak.

FIELD DIRECTIONS

1. Add nut butter and oil to the bag.

2. Massage bag with fingers or stir until well mixed.

3. Cut corner of bag and squeeze out or eat with a spoon.

HOME PREP

Mix Dry Ingred.

HOME PREP TIME

5 Min

FIELD PREP

No Cook

FIELD PREP TIME

3 Min

TOTAL SERVINGS

1

WEIGHT/ SERVING

5.3 oz

Nutrition Info PER SERVING	KCAL/OZ	CALORIES	PROTEIN	CARBS	FIBER	SUGAR	FAT
	152	806	21g	60g	13g	26g	60g

Download the Label File for

Chocoloate Almond Butter Snack

Directions: Add 1/4 cup (2 packets) almond or nut butter of choice and 1 Tbsp (1 packet) coconut oil to bag. Massage bag with fingers or stir with spoon. Coconut oil will mix better if warmed slightly by holding it in your hands or leaving it in the sunlight on a rock.

Ingredients: old fashioned oats, oat bran, chocolate chips, honey crystals

Nutrition: 806 kcal (152 kcal/oz), 21 g protein, 60 g carbohydrate, 13 g fiber, 26 g total sugars, 60 g fat

Net wt: 5.3 oz (including nut butter & oil)   **Exp. Date:** _____

www.backcountryfoodie.com

To download this label template, visit

https://www.backcountryfoodie.com/labels/chocolate-almond-butter-snack.pdf

or scan this barcode:

To find URL links for ingredients used, visit

https://backcountryfoodie.com/ingredients/

Berries & Nuts Trail Mix

INGREDIENTS

1 cup fancy mixed nuts

1/4 cup berries and cherries dehydrated fruit mix

2 Tbsp dark chocolate chips

Substitution:

Use carob chips for vegan option.

AT HOME DIRECTIONS

1. Put all ingredients in a bag or container to be used in the backcountry.

FIELD DIRECTIONS

1. Enjoy as is!

Note: Due to the presence of sunflower oil commonly found in fruit mixes, shelf life is uncertain as oil increases risk of rancidity

VEGETARIAN

VEGAN OPTION

GLUTEN-FREE

NO-COOK

HOME PREP

Mix Dry Ingred.

HOME PREP TIME

3 Min

FIELD PREP

No Cook

FIELD PREP TIME

Ready to Eat

TOTAL SERVINGS

1

WEIGHT/ SERVING

7.0 oz

	KCAL/OZ	CALORIES	PROTEIN	CARBS	FIBER	SUGAR	FAT
Nutrition Info PER SERVING	149	1044	26g	78g	13g	48g	81g

Download the Label File for

Berries & Nuts Trail Mix

Directions: Ready to eat!

Ingredients: mixed fancy nuts, blueberries, cherries, strawberries, cranberries, dark chocolate chips

Nutrition: 1044 kcal (149 kcal/oz), 26 g protein, 78 g carbohydrate, 13 g fiber, 48 g total sugars, 81 g fat

Net wt: 7 oz   Exp. Date: _____

www.backcountryfoodie.com

To download this label template, visit

https://www.backcountryfoodie.com/labels/berries-and-nuts-trail-mix.pdf

or scan this barcode:

To find URL links for ingredients used, visit

https://backcountryfoodie.com/ingredients/

The Foodie's Gorp

INGREDIENTS

3 Tbsp ancient grains granola

1/4 cup peanuts, unsalted

1/8 cup dried apricots, chopped

1/8 cup raisins

1/2 - 1.6 oz package peanut butter M&M's®

AT HOME DIRECTIONS

1. Put all ingredients in a bag or container to be used in the backcountry.

FIELD DIRECTIONS

2. Enjoy as is!

VEGETARIAN

NO-COOK

HOME PREP
Mix Dry Ingred.

HOME PREP TIME
5 Min

FIELD PREP
No Cook

FIELD PREP TIME
Ready to Eat

TOTAL SERVINGS
1

WEIGHT/ SERVING
4.0 oz

Nutrition Info PER SERVING	KCAL/OZ	CALORIES	PROTEIN	CARBS	FIBER	SUGAR	FAT
	127	509	14g	60g	8g	41g	27g

Download the Label File for

The Foodie's Gorp

Directions: Ready to eat!

Ingredients: ancient grains granola, peanuts, apricots, rasins, peanut butter M&M's®

Nutrition: 509 kcal (127 kcal/oz), 14 g protein, 59 g carbohydrate, 8 g fiber, 41 g total sugars, 27 g fat

Net wt: 4 oz   **Exp. Date:** _____

www.backcountryfoodie.com

To download this label template, visit

https://www.backcountryfoodie.com/labels/the-foodies-gorp.pdf

or scan this barcode:

To find URL links for ingredients used, visit

https://backcountryfoodie.com/ingredients/

DESSERTS

Double Chocolate Coconut Pudding

INGREDIENTS

20 chocolate animal crackers, without icing

1 - 3.56 oz box chocolate fudge instant pudding

1 cup shredded, unsweetened coconut

2/3 cup coconut milk powder

Substitution:

Use gluten-free cookies as a gluten-free alternative option.

AT HOME DIRECTIONS

1. Put animal crackers in a bowl and coarsely crush.
2. Add remaining ingredients to the bowl.
3. Stir to mix well.
4. Put 2.5 oz (1 serving) of mixture into four bags or containers to be used in the backcountry.

FIELD DIRECTIONS

1. Add 4 oz cold water to bag.
2. Shake vigorously until pudding thickens to desired consistency. This could take several minutes.
3. Stir and enjoy!

VEGETARIAN

GLUTEN-FREE OPTION

NUT-FREE

NO-COOK

HOME PREP
Mix Dry Ingred.

HOME PREP TIME
5 Min

FIELD PREP
No Cook

FIELD PREP TIME
10 Min

TOTAL SERVINGS
4

WEIGHT/ SERVING
2.5 oz

Nutrition Info PER SERVING	KCAL/OZ	CALORIES	PROTEIN	CARBS	FIBER	SUGAR	FAT
	138	345	5g	33g	4g	17g	24g

Download the Label File for

Double Chocolate Coconut Pudding

Directions: Add 4 oz cold water and shake vigorously until thickened to desired consistency. This can take several minutes. Stir and enjoy!

Ingredients: instant chocolate fudge pudding, coconut milk powder, unsweetened shredded coconut, chocolate animal crackers

Nutrition: 345 kcal (138 kcal/oz), 5 g protein, 33 g carbohydrate, 4 g fiber, 17 g total sugars, 24 g fat

Net wt: 2.5 oz   Exp. Date: _____

www.backcountryfoodie.com

To download this label template, visit

https://www.backcountryfoodie.com/labels/double-chocolate-coconut-pudding.pdf

or scan this barcode:

To find URL links for ingredients used, visit

https://backcountryfoodie.com/ingredients/

Peanut Butter Bananas Foster

INGREDIENTS

1 cup freeze-dried bananas

1 Tbsp unsweetened shredded coconut

2 Tbsp Emergency Essentials® peanut powder

2 Tbsp butter powder

1 Tbsp brown sugar

1/2 tsp cinnamon

1 packet True Lemon® powder

1 Tbsp coconut oil

Note: Recommend reading food labels and choosing full-fat peanut powders as many are designed to be low-fat.

AT HOME DIRECTIONS

1. Put all dry ingredients in a bag or container to be used in the backcountry.

2. Pack 1 Tbsp (1 – 0.5 oz packet) coconut oil, per serving, in a leakproof container to be added to the meal when consumed. Recommend double bagging the oil in the event there is a leak

FIELD DIRECTIONS

1. Add 4 oz hot water to bag.

2. Stir and let stand allowing bananas to rehydrate.

3. Add 1 Tbsp (1 – 0.5 oz packet) coconut oil.

4. Stir and enjoy!

HOME PREP

Mix Dry Ingred.

HOME PREP TIME

3 Min

FIELD PREP

Cook

FIELD PREP TIME

6 Min

TOTAL SERVINGS

1

WEIGHT/ SERVING

3.7 oz

Nutrition Info PER SERVING	KCAL/OZ	CALORIES	PROTEIN	CARBS	FIBER	SUGAR	FAT
	134	495	12g	57g	9g	46g	28g

Download the Label File for

Peanut Butter Bananas Foster

Directions: Add 4 oz hot water or to desired consistency. Let stand allowing bananas to rehydrate. Add 1 Tbsp (1 packet) coconut oil. Stir and enjoy!

Ingredients: bananas, shredded unsweetened coconut, peanut powder, brown sugar, butter powder, cinnamon, lemon powder

Nutrition: 495 kcal (134 kcal/oz), 12 g protein, 57 g carbohydrate, 9 g fiber, 46 g total sugars, 28 g fat

Net wt: 3.7 oz (including oil)   **Exp. Date:** _____

www.backcountryfoodie.com

To download this label template, visit

https://www.backcountryfoodie.com/labels/peanut-butter-bananas-foster.pdf

or scan this barcode:

To find URL links for ingredients used, visit

https://backcountryfoodie.com/ingredients/

Coconut Vanilla Bean Pudding

INGREDIENTS

20 vanilla bean wafers, crushed

1 - 3.5 oz package instant vanilla bean pudding

1 cup shredded, unsweetened coconut

2/3 cup whole milk powder

Substitution:

Use gluten-free cookies as a gluten-free alternative option.

AT HOME DIRECTIONS

1. Put vanilla wafers in a bowl and coarsely crush.
2. Add remaining ingredients to the bowl.
3. Stir to mix well.
4. Put 3.5 oz (1 serving) of mixture into four bags or containers to be used in the backcountry.

FIELD DIRECTIONS

1. Add 4 oz cold water to bag.
2. Shake vigorously until pudding thickens to desired consistency. This could take several minutes.
3. Stir and enjoy!

HOME PREP

Mix Dry Ingred.

HOME PREP TIME

5 Min

FIELD PREP

No Cook

FIELD PREP TIME

10 Min

TOTAL SERVINGS

4

WEIGHT/ SERVING

3.5 oz

	KCAL/OZ	CALORIES	PROTEIN	CARBS	FIBER	SUGAR	FAT
Nutrition Info PER SERVING	**128**	**449**	**7g**	**50g**	**3g**	**33g**	**25g**

Download the Label File for

Coconut Vanilla Bean Pudding

Directions: Add 4 oz cold water and shake vigorously until thickened to desired consistency. This can take several minutes. Stir and enjoy!

Ingredients: instant vanilla bean pudding, whole milk powder, unsweetened shredded coconut, vanilla bean wafers

Nutrition: 449 kcal (128 kcal/oz), 7 g protein, 50 g carbohydrate, 3 g fiber, 33 g total sugars, 25 g fat

Net wt: 3.5 oz   Exp. Date: _____

www.backcountryfoodie.com

To download this label template, visit

https://www.backcountryfoodie.com/labels/coconut-vanilla-bean-pudding.pdf

or scan this barcode:

To find URL links for ingredients used, visit

https://backcountryfoodie.com/ingredients/

BEVERAGES

Coconut Berry Smoothie

INGREDIENTS

1/2 cup freeze dried yogurt drops

1 cup freeze dried mixed berries

1/2 cup heavy cream powder

1 Tbsp shredded unsweetened coconut

AT HOME DIRECTIONS

1. Put all ingredients in a food processor and blend until yogurt is in powder form. Berries do not have to be blended into a fine powder.

2. Put powdered mix in a bag or container to be used in the backcountry

FIELD DIRECTIONS

1. Add 8 oz cold water or to desired consistency

2. Stir to mix well and enjoy!

VEG

GLUTEN-FREE

NUT-FREE

NO-COOK

HOME PREP
Mix Dry Ingred.

HOME PREP TIME
5 Min

FIELD PREP
No Cook

FIELD PREP TIME
2 Min

TOTAL SERVINGS
1

WEIGHT/ SERVING
3.6 oz

Nutrition **nfo** PER SERVING	KCAL/OZ	CALORIES	PROTEIN	CARBS	FIBER	SUGAR	FAT
	171	615	10g	89g	7g	49g	38g

Download the Label File for

Coconut Berry Smoothie

Directions: Add 8 oz cold water or to desired consistency. Stir and enjoy!

Ingredients: freeze dried yogurt, mixed berries, heavy cream powder, unsweetened shredded coconut

Nutrition: 615 kcal (171 kcal/oz), 10 g protein, 89 g carbohydrate, 7 g fiber, 49 g total sugars, 38 g fat

Net wt: 3.6 oz   **Exp. Date:** _____

www.backcountryfoodie.com

To download this label template, visit

https://www.backcountryfoodie.com/labels/coconut-berry-smoothie.pdf

or scan this barcode:

To find URL links for ingredients used, visit

https://backcountryfoodie.com/ingredients/

Coconut Ginger Milk

INGREDIENTS

1/4 cup whole milk powder

1 1/2 Tbsp coconut milk powder

1/2 Tbsp sugar

1/2 tsp ginger, ground

AT HOME DIRECTIONS

1. Put all ingredients in a bag or container to be used in the backcountry.

FIELD DIRECTIONS

1. Add 8 oz hot water or to desired flavor.
2. Stir and enjoy!

GLUTEN-FREE

NUT-FREE

COOK

HOME PREP
Mix Dry Ingred.

HOME PREP TIME
2 Min

FIELD PREP
Cook

FIELD PREP TIME
1 Min

TOTAL SERVINGS
1

WEIGHT/ SERVING
1.7 oz

	KCAL/OZ	CALORIES	PROTEIN	CARBS	FIBER	SUGAR	FAT
Nutrition Info PER SERVING	148	252	9g	20g	0g	18g	15g

Download the Label File for

Coconut Ginger Milk

Directions: Add 8 oz hot water or to desired flavor. Stir and enjoy!

Ingredients: whole milk powder, coconut milk powder, sugar, ginger

Nutrition: 252 kcal (148 kcal/oz), 9 g protein, 20 g carbohydrate, 0 g fiber, 18 g total sugars, 15 g fat

Net wt: 1.7 oz   Exp. Date: _____

www.backcountryfoodie.com

To download this label template, visit

https://www.backcountryfoodie.com/labels/coconut-ginger-milk.pdf

or scan this barcode:

To find URL links for ingredients used, visit

https://backcountryfoodie.com/ingredients/

Chai Latte

INGREDIENTS

1 Tbsp instant coffee

1/2 cup whole milk powder

2 Tbsp butter powder

2 tsp sugar

1/2 tsp ginger

1/2 tsp cinnamon

1/8 tsp cardamom

AT HOME DIRECTIONS

1. Put all ingredients in a bag or container to be used in the backcountry.

FIELD DIRECTIONS

1. Add 8 oz hot water or to desired flavor.

2. Stir and enjoy!

COOK

HOME PREP

Mix Dry Ingred.

HOME PREP TIME

2 Min

FIELD PREP

Cook

FIELD PREP TIME

1 Min

TOTAL SERVINGS

1

WEIGHT/ SERVING

3.0 oz

Nutrition **nfo** PER SERVING	KCAL/OZ	CALORIES	PROTEIN	CARBS	FIBER	SUGAR	FAT
	147	**442**	**16g**	**35g**	**<1g**	**33g**	**25g**

Download the Label File for

Chai Latte

Directions: Add 8 oz hot water or to desired flavor. Stir and enjoy!

Ingredients: instant coffee, whole milk powder, butter powder, sugar, ginger, cinnamon, cardamom

Nutrition: 442 kcal (147 kcal/oz), 16 g protein, 35 g carbohydrate, <1 g fiber, 33 g total sugars, 25 g fat

Net wt: 3 oz   **Exp. Date:** _____

www.backcountryfoodie.com

To download this label template, visit

https://www.backcountryfoodie.com/labels/chai-latte.pdf

or scan this barcode:

To find URL links for ingredients used, visit

https://backcountryfoodie.com/ingredients/

Tropical Delight Smoothie

INGREDIENTS

1/2 cup whole milk powder

1/2 cup freeze dried Greek yogurt

1/2 cup tropical blend freeze dried fruit

1 Tbsp unsweetened shredded coconut

AT HOME DIRECTIONS

1. Put all ingredients in a food processor and blend until yogurt is in powder form. Fruit does not have to be blended into a fine powder.

2. Put powdered mix in a bag or container to be used in the backcountry

FIELD DIRECTIONS

1. Add 8 oz cold water or to desired consistency.

2. Stir to mix well and enjoy!

VEGETARIAN

GLUTEN-FREE

NUT-FREE

NO-COOK

HOME PREP

Mix Dry Ingred.

HOME PREP TIME

5 Min

FIELD PREP

No Cook

FIELD PREP TIME

2 Min

TOTAL SERVINGS

1

WEIGHT/ SERVING

3.5 oz

	RCAL/OZ	CALORIES	PROTEIN	CARBS	FIBER	SUGAR	FAT
Nutrition nfo PER SERVING	143	499	17g	51g	2g	45g	25g

Download the Label File for

Tropical Delight Smoothie

Directions: Add 8 oz cold water or to desired consistency. Stir and enjoy!

Ingredients: whole milk powder, freeze dried Greek yogurt, tropical fruit blend, unsweetened shredded coconut

Nutrition: 499 kcal (143 kcal/oz), 17 g protein, 51 g carbohydrate, 2 g fiber, 45 g total sugars, 25 g fat

Net wt: 3.5 oz   Exp. Date: _____

www.backcountryfoodie.com

To download this label template, visit

https://www.backcountryfoodie.com/labels/tropical-delight-smoothie.pdf

or scan this barcode:

To find URL links for ingredients used, visit

https://backcountryfoodie.com/ingredients/

White Chocolate Hot Chocolate

INGREDIENTS

1/2 cup whole milk powder

1 Tbsp cocoa powder

1 tsp sugar

1/8 cup white chocolate chips

AT HOME DIRECTIONS

1. Put all ingredients in a bag or container to be used in the backcountry.

FIELD DIRECTIONS

1. Add 6 oz hot water or to desired flavor.

2. Stir and enjoy!

VEGETARIAN

GLUTEN-FREE

NUT-FREE

COOK

HOME PREP

Mix Dry Ingred.

HOME PREP TIME

2 Min

FIELD PREP

Cook

FIELD PREP TIME

1 Min

TOTAL SERVINGS

1

WEIGHT/ SERVING

3.5 oz

	KCAL/OZ	CALORIES	PROTEIN	CARBS	FIBER	SUGAR	FAT
Nutrition nfo PER SERVING	**142**	**498**	**17g**	**47g**	**1g**	**44g**	**27g**

Download the Label File for

White Chocolate Hot Chocolate

Directions: Add 6 oz hot water or to desired flavor. Stir and enjoy!

Ingredients: whole milk powder, cocoa powder, sugar, white chocolate chips

Nutrition: 498 kcal (142 kcal/oz), 17 g protein, 47 g carbohydrate, 1 g fiber, 44 g total sugars, 27 g fat

Net wt: 3.5 oz   **Exp. Date:** _____

www.backcountryfoodie.com

To download this label template, visit

https://www.backcountryfoodie.com/labels/white-chocolate-hot-chocolate.pdf

or scan this barcode:

To find URL links for ingredients used, visit

https://backcountryfoodie.com/ingredients/

Hazelnut Almond Coffee

INGREDIENTS

1 Tbsp instant coffee

3 Tbsp hazelnut and almond powder

2 Tbsp heavy cream powder

1/2 tsp sugar

Note: A variety of nut powders can oftentimes be found at Asian markets.

AT HOME DIRECTIONS

1. Put all ingredients in a bag or container to be used in the backcountry.

FIELD DIRECTIONS

1. Add 6 oz hot water or to desired flavor.

2. Stir and enjoy!

VEGETARIAN

GLUTEN-FREE

COOK

HOME PREP
Mix Dry Ingred.

HOME PREP TIME
2 Min

FIELD PREP
Cook

FIELD PREP TIME
1 Min

TOTAL SERVINGS
1

WEIGHT/ SERVING
1.6 oz

Nutrition Info PER SERVING	KCAL/OZ	CALORIES	PROTEIN	CARBS	FIBER	SUGAR	FAT
	141	226	2g	26g	2g	6g	13g

Download the Label File for

Hazelnut Almond Coffee

Directions: Add 6 oz hot water or to desired flavor. Stir and enjoy!

Ingredients: instant coffee, hazelnut and almond powder, heavy cream powder, sugar

Nutrition: 226 kcal (141 kcal/oz), 2 g protein, 26 g carbohydrate, 2 g fiber, 6 g total sugars, 13 g fat

Net wt: 1.6 oz   Exp. Date: _____

www.backcountryfoodie.com

To download this label template, visit

https://www.backcountryfoodie.com/labels/hazelnut-almond-coffee.pdf

or scan this barcode:

To find URL links for ingredients used, visit

https://backcountryfoodie.com/ingredients/

Peppermint Latte

INGREDIENTS

1 Tbsp instant coffee

1/4 cup whole milk powder

2 hard peppermint candies, crushed

AT HOME DIRECTIONS

1. Put peppermint candies in a spice mill and grind into a powder.

2. Put all ingredients in a bag or container to be used in the backcountry.

FIELD DIRECTIONS

1. Add 8 oz hot water or to desired flavor.

2. Stir and enjoy!

GLUTEN-FREE

NUT-FREE

COOK

HOME PREP

Mix Dry Ingred.

HOME PREP TIME

3 Min

FIELD PREP

Cook

FIELD PREP TIME

1 Min

TOTAL SERVINGS

1

WEIGHT/ SERVING

1.5 oz

Nutrition Info PER SERVING	KCAL/OZ	CALORIES	PROTEIN	CARBS	FIBER	SUGAR	FAT
	141	211	7g	23g	0g	18g	21g

113

Download the Label File for

Peppermint Latte

Directions: Add 8 oz hot water or to desired flavor. Stir and enjoy!

Ingredients: instant coffee, whole milk powder, peppermint candies

Nutrition: 211 kcal (141 kcal/oz), 7 g protein, 23 g carbohydrate, 0 g fiber, 18 g total sugars, 21 g fat

Net wt: 1.5 oz   Exp. Date: _____

www.backcountryfoodie.com

To download this label template, visit

https://www.backcountryfoodie.com/labels/peppermint-latte.pdf

or scan this barcode:

To find URL links for ingredients used, visit

https://backcountryfoodie.com/ingredients/

Vanilla Spiced Milk

INGREDIENTS

1/3 cup whole milk powder

1 tsp vanilla powder

1 tsp sugar

1/2 tsp cinnamon

1/4 tsp nutmeg

AT HOME DIRECTIONS

1. Put all ingredients in a bag or container to be used in the backcountry.

FIELD DIRECTIONS

1. Add 8 oz hot/cold water or to desired flavor.

2. Stir and enjoy!

VEGETARIAN

GLUTEN-FREE

NUT-FREE

COOK

NO-COOK

HOME PREP
Mix Dry Ingred.

HOME PREP TIME
3 Min

FIELD PREP
Cook, No Cook

FIELD PREP TIME
1 Min

TOTAL SERVINGS
1

WEIGHT/ SERVING
1.9 oz

	KCAL/OZ	CALORIES	PROTEIN	CARBS	FIBER	SUGAR	FAT
Nutrition Info PER SERVING	138	262	11g	21g	.8g	20g	14g

Download the Label File for

Vanilla Spiced Milk

Directions: Add 8 oz hot/cold water or to desired flavor. Stir and enjoy!

Ingredients: whole milk powder, vanilla powder, cinnamon, nutmeg, sugar

Nutrition: 262 kcal (138 kcal/oz), 11 g protein, 21 g carbohydrate, 0.8 g fiber, 20 g total sugars, 14 g fat

Net wt: 1.9 oz   **Exp. Date:** _____

www.backcountryfoodie.com

To download this label template, visit

https://www.backcountryfoodie.com/labels/vanilla-spiced-milk.pdf

or scan this barcode:

To find URL links for ingredients used, visit

https://backcountryfoodie.com/ingredients/

Chocolate Peanut Butter Milk

INGREDIENTS

1/3 cup whole milk powder

1 packet Carnation Breakfast Essentials® powder, chocolate

3 Tbsp Emergency Essentials® peanut powder

Note: Recommend reading food labels and choosing full-fat peanut powders as many are designed to be low-fat.

AT HOME DIRECTIONS

1. Put all ingredients in a bag or container to be used in the backcountry.

FIELD DIRECTIONS

1. Add 8 oz cold water or to desired flavor.
1. Stir or shake vigorously to mix well. Massage bag with fingertips if peanut powder clumps.
1. Enjoy!

VEGETARIAN

GLUTEN-FREE

NO-COOK

HOME PREP

Mix Dry Ingred.

HOME PREP TIME

3 Min

FIELD PREP

No Cook

FIELD PREP TIME

2 Min

TOTAL SERVINGS

1

WEIGHT/ SERVING

3.4 oz

	KCAL/OZ	CALORIES	PROTEIN	CARBS	FIBER	SUGAR	FAT
Nutrition Info PER SERVING	129	440	23g	47g	3g	36g	18g

Download the Label File for

Chocolate Peanut Butter Milk

Directions: Add 8 oz cold water or to desired flavor. Shake vigorously and/or massage bag with fingertips if peanut butter clumps are present. Stir and enjoy!

Ingredients: Carnation Breakfast Essentials® milk chocolate powder, whole milk powder, peanut powder

Nutrition: 440 kcal (129 kcal/oz), 23 g protein, 47 g carbohydrate, 3 g fiber, 36 g total sugars,18 g fat

Net wt: 3.4 oz   **Exp. Date:** _____

www.backcountryfoodie.com

To download this label template, visit

https://www.backcountryfoodie.com/labels/chocolate-peanut-butter-milk.pdf

or scan this barcode:

To find URL links for ingredients used, visit

https://backcountryfoodie.com/ingredients/

Index

Cherries, dried

  berries & nuts trail mix 87

  sweet & savory couscous 79

Cherries, freeze-dried

  cherry almond milk oatmeal 19

Cherry Almond Milk Oatmeal 19

Chili powder

  sweet & savory couscous 79

Chips & Salsa with Guacamole 47

Chocolate

  berries & nuts trail mix 87

  candies in the foodie's gorp 89

  chocolate almond butter snack 85

  chocolate peanut butter milk 117

  double chocolate coconut pudding 93

  white chocolate hot chocolate 109

Chocolate Almond Butter Snack 85

Chocolate chips, dark

  berries & nuts trail mix 87

  chocolate almond butter snack 85

Chocolate chips, white

  white chocolate hot chocolate 109

Chocolate Peanut Butter Milk 117

Cinnamon

  chai latte 105

  vanilla spiced milk 115

Citrus Pecan Cream Cheese 11

Cocoa powder

  white chocolate hot chocolate 109

Coconut Berry Smoothie 101

Coconut Ginger Milk 103

Coconut milk powder

  coconut ginger milk 103

  double chocolate coconut pudding 93

  fruity breakfast grits 17

  Thai peanut ramen 39

Coconut, shredded unsweetened

  coconut berry smoothie 101

  coconut vanilla bean pudding 97

  double chocolate coconut pudding 93

  peanut butter bananas foster 95

  strawberry coconut almond oatmeal 25

  tropical delight smoothie 107

Coconut Vanilla Bean Pudding 97

M

N

Ultralight Recipes for Outdoor Explorers

BACKCOUNTRY FOODIE

Creation of Backcountry Foodie - Ultralight Meal Planning for Outdoor Explorers

After 17 years as a clinical dietitian, Aaron decided to combine her athletic and professional passions to start the Backcountry Foodie LLC, which officially launched in January of 2018. As the Backcountry Foodie, she develops ultralight meal plans for avid outdoor explorers just like herself. Aaron saw a need to develop these meal plans as a result of her own fear that she would lose an excessive amount of weight while thru hiking. As a dietitian with expert nutrition knowledge, creation of Backcountry Foodie was the perfect solution allowing her to share her own personal experiences with those that also desire a nutritionally adequate diet while in the backcountry.

Visit www.backcountryfoodie.com for more details about the ultralight meal planning services that Aaron provides.

CPSIA information can be obtained
at www.ICGtesting.com
Printed in the USA
LVHW082311021118
595834LV00010B/66/P